MW00941313

# Finding Joy
# In The Journey

## Dealing With Terminal Illness

*Our Family Story of Discovering the
Goodness of God in Times of Suffering*

# *Vickie Tingwald*

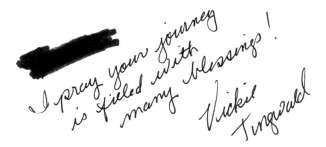

I pray your journey is filled with many blessings! Vickie Tingwald

Copyright © 2021 Vickie Tingwald
All rights reserved
First Edition

PAGE PUBLISHING, INC.
Conneaut Lake, PA

First originally published by Page Publishing 2021

ISBN 978-1-6624-3238-5 (pbk)
ISBN 978-1-6624-3239-2 (digital)

Printed in the United States of America

THIS BOOK IS dedicated to the memory of my husband and forever love, Gary Tingwald. He will always remain my hero, best friend, and the greatest example of Christ I have ever known. He told me before he died that he wanted me to "find joy in the journey" after he was gone. His love and the love of our heavenly Father has made that possible. I would also like to dedicate the book to my children and grandchildren who were by my husband's side every step of the way and made forever stronger in Christ because of our family's journey through suffering.

# Contents

# Introduction

IN WRITING THIS book, my first reason was to record the goodness of God so that our family would never forget what God had done for us in our darkest hours. It was to help my children and grandchildren remember the faith and courage of their father and grandfather. But my greatest reason in writing this book was to give glory and honor to my God for all he has done and continues to do in our lives.

Somewhere in the writing and recording, God changed my direction. I want my family to remember because I know, as they run the race for Christ, these remembrances will strengthen their faith and give them the courage they need to finish the race. As my writing progressed, God gave me a much larger mandate. Along with all my own reasons, God impressed upon my heart that the body of Christ needs to know about suffering and how to be victorious in this life. One of the greatest needs in our preaching today is that the body of Christ is not being prepared for suffering. As the time of Christ's return draws near, we will need to be strong and courageous. It takes courage to endure pain; we witnessed that courage in my husband's life.

Look at two lives in God's Word that are our examples. The first is Paul and the second is Christ. Both suffered untold agonies for us to know the truth. Paul was beaten on three occasions with rods, beaten by the Jews five times, given thirty-nine lashes, stoned, shipwrecked three times, abandoned, given a thorn in the flesh, thrown in prison, put in chains, and was on house arrest. These are only some of the things that Paul endured for the sake of the gospel. Paul wanted to encourage the Christians to be courageous and strong in a time when they were being persecuted and killed by the Romans. He wanted them to know that to suffer for Christ was a small price to pay for their eternal salvation. Paul taught that to suffer for Christ's sake was an honor.

Then there is the suffering that our Lord had to endure. He suffered everything we would have to suffer. He endured physical, emotional, and spiritual trauma for us. He took it all on himself on the cross. He was arrested, beaten until pieces of his flesh were torn from his body, tortured, ridiculed, thought crazy by his own family, denied by the ones who knew him most, mocked, falsely tried and accused, made to carry his own cross, and so much more. His greatest suffering was perhaps, as he hung on the cross, his Father turning his back on him because of our sins. Christ then cried out, "Father, why have you forsaken me?" That separation and loneliness was the greatest agony of all.

As we think about our Lord and Paul, how can we not realize that we, too, will suffer for the sake of the gospel? When we give our lives to Christ, our enemy, Satan, does not like it, and he begins his assault on us. God wants us to be ready and know that greater is he that is in us than he who is in the world. He wants us to know that we are more than conquerors in this life, right now! The only way we will be prepared when suffering comes, and it will come to us all, is to know God and know his Word. That is the message God wants you to know, and he has asked me to tell you.

In the pages of this book, you will read about *victory* over defeat. You will see real people fighting real battles for their lives. And you will see how one man was victorious and remained courageous through the battle of terminal illness. It is my prayer that you will be challenged to live a life of courage and strength. I pray you will have a desire to see life through eternal perspective and store up your treasures in heaven. A life where your priorities place God and his Word first and foremost in your daily walk. But most of all, that as you read with an open heart and mind, you would learn and understand that our great God is as sufficient in times of trials as he is in the times of joy. In him you can "find joy in the journey!"

# CHAPTER 1

*We All Have A Story To Tell*

> You make known to me the path of life; in your presence there is fullness of joy; at your right hand are pleasures forevermore.
>
> —Psalm 16:11

## This Is Our Story

HAVE YOU EVER had more questions than answers in dealing with the struggles of life? How can a loving God allow this to happen? What purpose does this trial serve in my life? What good can ever come out of this situation? Is God listening to me or does he even care? What about the apostle Paul telling us to count it all joy, do you believe that is even possible? How do you handle the trials of life? Do you confront them with a "blame game" attitude or you might be that person who has a need for an explanation, a reason for everything that happens in life? It is human nature to want to know why or try to make sense out of the circumstance you now face. But what do you do when there are no answers, no one to blame, or a way to explain or even understand why? Sometimes, the things of this life just do not seem to make sense or have any obvious purpose! Then where do you go, what do you do?

This book was not written to be the answers to all your questions or as an expert expose on suffering. It was written to bring encouragement and hope when you are going through difficult crossroads in life. Also, to remind us that our victory has already been purchased through the precious blood of our Savior, Jesus Christ! To God be the glory in every word of this book.

## Our Family's ALS Journey

Our family experienced a roller coaster ride of emotions when my perfectly healthy husband of fifty years was diagnosed with ALS, also known as Lou Gehrig's disease. ALS is a terminal illness with no treatment or cure. The only hope you have is to manage the symptoms, and ALS has a plethora of symptoms. My precious husband endured over seven years of suffering and losing all his bodily functions. He was trapped in a useless body but left with a beautiful mind and spirit. We asked ourselves and God all the questions of why and for what purpose but found no answers.

## We Can Rejoice

"Rejoice in the Lord always and again
I say rejoice!" (Philippians 4:4)

Out of the ashes of pain and torment, our family discovered the mystery of how to rejoice during the suffering. I believe the lessons our family learned on our journey will help give you some clarity and peace with whatever trial you are facing. We also want to give God all the glory for the mysteries he unlocked for us as a family, and in our individual journeys of coping with the grief of a terminal illness.

In writing this book, I have tried to give a voice to the suffering of each member of our family. A terminal illness is a family affair, and we all had personal journeys of discovery and spiritual growth.

In the chapters of this book, you will hear from several members of our family, my husband's thoughts as well.

My hope is that in reading about our suffering, you will know that you are not alone, you will learn about how God showed himself strong to us and how he was always right there with us, every step of the way. I pray you will gain the knowledge of God's Word needed to walk in faith and not fear when facing your giants. And most important of all, that you will realize that we all will suffer at some time in our life, the question is not *if* but *when*, and if we know that, we will be more prepared when the time comes. Knowledge is power, power to overcome the difficult trials of this journey called life and our daily battles with the enemy of our soul.

After my husband passed away, God began to speak to me about writing down what our family had learned over the last seven years. In the Word of God, we are encouraged over and over to remember the things God has done for us. I wanted my family to remember how God brought us through the most difficult and darkest time of our life victorious and stronger! I have always journaled, so recording my thoughts was not hard, in fact, it helped me to cope with my grief. But as time passed, God's voice grew louder, and I felt a sense of urgency in what he wanted me to tell the body of Christ. It became more about sharing our journey to help others. He was speaking to my grieving heart about writing a book.

At first, I liked the idea because, like I said, I enjoy writing. I thought it would be a way to record all that God had done for us so that the next generation of my family would always remember and know the goodness of our God. The voice of God's Spirit was continually asking me to take another step of faith. I felt like Peter when Christ told him to step out of the boat. God is always asking us to stretch our faith so that we will need to draw ever closer and depend on him. So, now the journal has become a book to be published. True to my nature, I debated with God that I was not an author and knew nothing about writing a book. It was one thing to write things down for my family but another to record our private pain for others to read about. Then God reminded me that he does not ask us to be obedient based on our abilities but on what he can do through us.

God asks us to do the things that are beyond our talents and abilities because when it is accomplished, we will know that it was only because of God in us working through us.

I knew not to tell too many people because often, people, unknowingly, tend to discourage your dreams. So, I only told those that I knew would get behind me and pray for my success and for God to be glorified. I needed to trust and tell a few people so I would have some accountability. My journey had begun, and I would need to trust God to guide and direct me if I were to succeed. This was one of those God-ordained assignments I knew would only get completed with God's help. I suddenly could relate to how Noah must have felt when given such a monumental task as building an ark. And, of course, Moses when God asked him to be the spokesperson and leader of the nation of Israel. That was no small task because records tell us that at the time of their exodus, there were an estimated two million people that Moses would be responsible for, that was not counting other family members and livestock.

My point is that God never asks us to do small things that we can accomplish on our own. Now, do not get me wrong, God wants us to be faithful in the small things and then he will ask us to do the more difficult things. The word of God tells us in Zachariah 4:10 to never be ashamed of small beginnings. He wants to challenge and grow our faith by asking us to do things that we know we could never accomplish on our own, then he will be glorified. God wants us to dream big when it comes to his kingdom and telling others about what an awesome God we serve. It should never be about what we have done but always about what God has done. All glory and honor are his alone.

## The Diagnosis of ALS

My husband was given a terminal diagnosis in June of 2012 when after a year of tests, we were told he had ALS, which stands for amyotrophic lateral sclerosis, also known as Lou Gehrig's disease. ALS is a motor neuron disease that causes the death of the nerve cells that extend from the brain to the spinal cord and muscles throughout the body. It is considered a rare neurological disease that causes the body to lose control over the major voluntary muscles that produce movements like chewing, swallowing, walking, talking, and even breathing. Only about 30,000 people in the US have ALS in any given year because they are dying in three to five years of their diagnosis. In the world of diseases, that is a small number, so it is considered a rare disease with an estimated 5,000 new cases each year in the US. But if it affects your family, it does not feel rare or small! ALS is most likely to develop in Caucasians and non-Hispanics in the age range of 55–75. Men are slightly more likely to develop ALS than women. Men who have served in the military are about 2 percent more likely to develop ALS than men who have not been in the military. ALS is recognized as a service-connected disease by the US Department of Veterans Affairs. Veterans who are diagnosed with ALS are immediately considered 100 percent disabled.

ALS is considered either sporadic or familiar. Sporadic ALS is the most common, found in 90 percent of those diagnosed. Familiar ALS is found in only about 5 to 10 percent of the population. Familiar ALS means the person has inherited the disease from a parent. It only requires one parent to carry the gene responsible for ALS. Mutations in more than a dozen genes have been found to cause familiar ALS. About 25–40 percent of all familiar ALS cases are caused by a defect in a gene known as "chromosome 9 or C9ORF72." This same mutation is associated with atrophy of the frontal-temporal lobes of the brain. In familiar ALS, the frontal-temporal lobes of the brain can be affected and cause frontal lobe dementia.

ALS has no cure and no effective treatments to halt or reverse the progression of the disease. It takes a year to be diagnosed because there is no test for ALS at this time. ALS is diagnosed through a process of testing and ruling out everything else it could be. Usually, by the time you're diagnosed, you have a fairly good idea of what your future holds. But we always held on to hope of a better diagnosis until the day we got the call and heard the words, "Sorry, Mrs. Tingwald, your husband has been diagnosed with Bulbar ALS." My husband, who was just sixty years old, a father, grandfather, and a man who loved the Lord, and served his country heroically in Vietnam, was given a death sentence that day. He was given less than three years to live. In most ALS cases, you are given 3–5 years, but "Bulbar" ALS is its own beast, we were to find out. It attacks your diaphragm, breathing and swallowing with a vengeance.

In writing this book, my purpose is threefold. First, to give glory to our heavenly Father who never leaves us and who carries us when we can no longer take another step on our own. Second, to help and encourage those who are in the battle of their life right now. It could be a struggle with your health, finances, marriage, children, or any number of trials we all face daily. But I believe that God has, and is, the answer you are looking for. And finally, to help you unlock the mystery of God's Word concerning suffering as followers of Christ. It is about finding the "joy in the journey." Our love for God never shines any brighter than when we are being tested. And it is in the testing that our character and strength are developed by God. Strength for whatever, God alone knows, lies ahead.

> "Blessed is the man who perseveres under
> trial, because when he has stood the test, he
> will receive the crown of life to that God has
> promised to those who love him." (James 1: 12)

Please, let this book guide you on your search of truth and discovery of just how good our heavenly Father is when we surrender our lives and trust him each step of the way. Our family has forever been changed by God's mercy and grace. We have learned to not only survive but to thrive while in the battle as we allow God to teach us and change us from glory to glory. We certainly are not experts, but our hope is that in the telling of our story, you will be drawn to Jesus Christ, the one who is the answer to all our questions.

I pray you are comforted by God's love, presence, and peace as you journey through this life. Remembering that the goal of our faith is always our salvation that was purchased by the precious blood of Jesus Christ. We all have a story to tell and this is ours.

This is my story, this is my song
Praising my Savior all the day long
This is my story, this is my song
Praising my Savior all the day long

## "ALS—A Family Affair" by Melissa Tingwald-Alvarez

When asked to speak at the ALS symposium in Washington, DC, this is how our youngest daughter, Melissa, told her story.

The great Lou Gehrig and my dad, Gary Tingwald, have a lot in common. I know you are thinking, ALS. But that is just one of the many things they share. Lou Gehrig was known as the "Iron Horse" because of his endurance and strength. My dad is the strongest man that I have ever known. My dad is a Vietnam veteran, retired prison chaplain, spent time in Haiti as an electrician, and wood craftsman. He has always been physically strong, but ALS robbed him of these things. ALS is constantly taking away his physical strength, but it will never take away his inner strength.

It was while on a family trip to Disneyworld in 2011 when we first noticed subtle changes in my dad. He was slurring his speech and choking on his food. When we got home, he went to his doctor. After a stroke was ruled out, he went through about a year of testing. Although we prayed and hoped against an ALS diagnosis, we knew the signs. That is because my family is no stranger to ALS. My dad is the fourth male in his family to receive this diagnosis. And because of that, we already had a glimpse of what life with ALS would be like. As my dad's cousin, Tim, was already losing his battle with the disease when my dad's battle had just begun.

In three short months, my dad lost his voice and was forced to retire from a career he loved. As a pastor, his voice was a major part of his profession. That is one thing I really miss, the sound of my dad's voice. Some days, I would call to listen to his voice mail recording just to hear the sound of his voice again. A few months later, he began having difficulty eating and was put on a feeding tube. Imagine smelling popcorn at a movie theater, hot dogs at a baseball game, or hot apple pie at Thanksgiving and not being able to eat a big piece.

Finally, just a year ago, my dad's breathing began to weaken. After months of research and family discussions, he made the decision to receive a trach tube. My dad used to teach me softball, run with the grandkids, build furniture, play sports, and led an active lifestyle. Now, just three years after his diagnosis, he is in a wheelchair, eats through a feeding tube, and sleeps hooked up to a ventilator. It is a heartbreaking, painful thing to watch this happen to your loved one. But as in all of life, we have choices. My dad could have chosen to stay home and just give up, but that is not my dad. He is facing life with ALS head on. His determination has kept him and my mom traveling, going to sporting events, and simply doing all the things they love to do. The day-to-day strength of both my mom and dad is simply inspiring.

ALS did not just happen to my dad, it happened to our entire family, and we chose to rally behind him and Mom to make the best of this awful situation. Although our family is spread apart in three states, we all make the effort to help and support them as much as possible.

My dad requires someone with him all day; although he has a nurse for a few hours a day, my mom is his primary caregiver. If you know someone who is a caregiver, you understand the exhausting task that it can be. Mundane tasks like showering, shaving, dressing, getting in and out of the car, and so much more require extra hands at times. I cannot even imagine the pain that my mom is going through to see her husband of forty-seven years battle ALS. She willingly makes many sacrifices to care for my dad. She can no longer live a carefree life of retirement. But my mom would not have it any other way—she has been by his side every agonizing step of the way. I can see the love my mom has for my dad in so many ways: as she guides him to the shower, as she cleans his trach tube, as she helps him dress, as she crawls into their van to hook down dad's wheelchair, as she is always sure that he is comfortable, and as she gives up time with her family and friends just to spend her time with my dad. It can be very demanding, caring for someone with ALS, but her commitment to my dad is unwavering.

I have three siblings, and all of us try to help as much as possible. I have learned to set up my dad's feeding bags, clean his trach, suction him, and so many more things I never imagined I would have to do. We know that one day we may not be able to provide all the care that he needs. Eventually, he will need a nurse full time. But until then, we are all changing our lives and schedules to help as much as we can. This is what family does when faced with illness. We are all working to get through this together.

Through all he has been through, my dad still has a quick wit and sarcasm. And plenty of it! He now must use a speech program on his iPad to communicate with us. When we see him typing as fast as he can, we know he is getting ready to tell us a joke. His spirit has never changed.

They say that ALS feels like being trapped in your own body, and my dad tells us that is true. We are happy that he is still able to interact with us, just in new ways. For my dad and family, I will be relentless in helping to find a cure for ALS and to give hope to other families facing the same battle as our family. I am honored to be here tonight, telling you my story. I will not stop telling this story until there is a cure for the horrific disease. I want to thank you all for your continued support of the ALS Association. I have been afforded to see the good that they are doing, firsthand. I volunteer at the Rockville, Maryland, office, cleaning and organizing their donation closet. Living with ALS is extremely costly. Fortunately, my dad has benefits with the Veteran's Association, but not every ALS family has this benefit. The equipment needed to live daily with ALS is expensive. The donation closet that I help with allows people with ALS to come and borrow or receive at no cost the much needed supplies. They have everything from food, medical supplies, everyday devices to help make life easier, to wheelchairs. These supplies can make a huge difference in someone's life.

My family is also involved in the ALS support group in Virginia, where my parents live. This support group, sponsored by their local ALS Association, is like family to us. My parents have received so much help and support from them. As a matter of fact, my family recently rented a suite at the baseball stadium and invited a few of their ALS friends to the game in celebration of my dad's birthday! When facing this ALS journey, it is vitally important to have people beside you that know and understand your struggles.

My family finds us in an ALS minority. We are one of the 5 to 10 percent of ALS patients that have familiar ALS. That means that because my dad has familiar ALS, my siblings and I have a 50 percent chance of inheriting the gene that may develop into ALS. As a sister, an aunt to five nephews, and mother of three, I will stop at nothing to help eradicate this disease. I try not to worry about statistics or let my mind think of the "what ifs." But it would be ignoring reality to do so. The likelihood of having another family member diagnosed with ALS is high, but I believe that through more funding and research, we will not have to see ALS take the life of another member of my family. I would have never imagined that one day I would be standing here tonight giving a speech on ALS. But I will keep speaking for my dad's uncle Howard Tingwald, his uncle Don Tingwald, his cousin Tim Tingwald, and my dad, Gary Tingwald. I will keep speaking for those in the ALS community that do not have a voice because of this disease. And I will speak for future generations of my family and our ALS family.

So, if you dumped a bucket of ice water over your head, thank you. If you have walked to defeat ALS, thank you. And thank you for being here tonight. Every video of someone doing the "Ice Bucket Challenge" brought tears to my eyes. Those of us loving and caring for a person with ALS, thank you. You have helped to bring ALS out into the light. Now, when I tell someone that my dad has ALS, they understand and recognize the disease more. To have ALS in the spotlight brings hope and encouragement to us all.

In Lou Gehrig's farewell speech, he spoke his famous line, "I might have been given a bad break, but I have an awful lot to live for." My dad lives the same sentiment. We know that ALS is really a bad break, but my dad's optimism in the face of ALS is inspiring. Thank you for listening to my story tonight. I hope I gave you a glimpse into life with ALS. My dad's life is not defined by ALS, it is defined by all the good that he has done throughout his life. My dad will always be the strongest, most inspiring person that I know. As I was preparing this speech, I asked my dad what his favorite quote is. He said, "You can judge the size of the victory by the size of the battle." I thought this would be a perfect quote for us tonight. It may seem like a huge battle to find a cure for ALS, but when we do, what a massive victory it will be!

# CHAPTER 2

## *A True Foundation*

For no one can lay any foundation other than the
one already laid, which is Jesus Christ.
—1 Corinthians 3:11

### Our Lives Are Like Puzzles

OUR LIVES ARE like one giant puzzle with thousands of pieces.
When we are putting a puzzle together, we want the pieces to go
together easily and fit perfectly. Other times, we search and search
to find the right piece, and it seems impossible. And then there are
the times when you get the puzzle all completed, but there is a missing or lost piece. It can be frustrating. Life can be like that puzzle.
Sometimes in our lives that lost piece represents a question we know
will never be answered in this life. God holds the pieces of our life,
and if we will allow him, he will fit each piece exactly when and
where it belongs to make something beautiful out of our life. But
that requires placing our faith and trust in his hands. When we trust
God, he will give us that "true foundation" we need for all of life.

In the book of Matthew, the seventh chapter, we see an example
of two lives, one built on a sure foundation of rock and the other

built on sinking sand. In this illustration, God is giving us a warning that if we are to withstand the storms of life, we need a solid foundation. Jesus Christ is that solid foundation we must build on.

> "Therefore, everyone who hears these words
> of mine and puts them into practice is like
> a wise man who built his house on the rock.
> The rain came down, the streams rose,
> and the winds blew and beat against the
> house, yet it did not fall because it had its
> foundation on the rock." (Matthew 7:24–25)

## Do Not Be Caught Off Guard

For a long time, I believed that just because I lived my life serving God, he would take care of me and my family and nothing bad would happen to us. I mean look, I have paid my tithe faithfully, served on every committee when asked, taught Sunday school and children's church. I even became a minister, and so did my husband. We went on mission trips. That should all count for something. God will surely take care of us because we have done so much for him. I guess I thought God could not run the universe without me! Then as life often does, things did not go the way I thought they should, and I begin to question my faith in God.

Like so many others when trials came to our family, I was caught off guard and left questioning God with all my "whys." And if I were to be honest, I was disappointed and angry with God at times. I guess I still had not learned that God's ways are higher than ours, and we need to trust him. I had a lot of spiritual growing to do in the area of trust. But let me go back a few years and give you a look into our lives so you know how God had us exactly where we needed to be when this tragedy struck.

## Gary's New Assignment from God

All through my life, I have approached God with a childlike faith and tried to do my best to be obedient, never perfectly but always making the attempt. That was until the day my husband told me that God was calling him to be an institutional chaplain. My response was, "You mean to prisons and jails?" He responded, "Yes." And I said, "Not with this wife!"

My rebellious reaction and response shocked both of us! I did not understand my own reaction or why I was so against this new assignment from God. I knew my husband well enough, after thirty-five years of marriage, to know that he had heard from God. But somehow, this just did not compute in my brain. Where did I fit in jail ministry? I was a children's pastor! It meant we would be starting over again. Thankfully, both God and Gary were patient with me and waited for me to come around. I am ashamed to say it took me about two years of arguing with God (which, as you know, is always a losing battle) and soul-searching. I think I knew from the moment Gary had told me that he had heard from God, but I was frightened by the huge change it would make in our life. As I look back, I am amazed at God and Gary's love for me and their patience. Who was I to question God and his plan for our lives? I thought I trusted God, but I began to question where I was in my walk of faith.

After a lot of prayer and discussion with God, I came around. But I was honest with God and told him my faith just was not where it needed to be for what he was asking. Then I said, "God, you are going to have to show yourself strong on our behalf in order for me to be up to this new challenge." I can honestly say, from the moment of that prayer, God began to show himself strong and continues to this very day! God is so gracious with us, his children. Like our earthly parents, if they are wise, God allows us to make mistakes and is still faithful in his love and patience with us. How frustrating it must be for God as he watches us trying to maintain control instead of leaning on and trusting him. God knows our future, so why do we struggle so much trying to tell him what *we think* is best? And so, the next chapter of our lives began, and we announced to our church that we would be leaving for the chaplaincy. Since we were both on staff there, the church lost two pastors.

## Counting the Cost

In our denomination, the chaplaincy is considered US missions. This means that you must raise all your own support. When we left our position as pastors at our church, we gave up our home that was owned by the church. We walked away from home, paycheck, health insurance, and family to start over. Leaving family was hardest on me. Our two daughters lived close by, and our youngest daughter had just had our first granddaughter. We were living in the Washington, DC, area and because housing and the cost of living was so high there and we needed to be more centrally located in our church district for travel, we moved to Chesapeake, Virginia. There is always something to be thankful for, our oldest daughter lived there with our two grandsons. Bonus!

We had started over, it seemed, so many times in our lives, but this time seemed to be more difficult for me. I think because it was an entirely different career path and because of our age. We were now in our midforties, and this would be our *fourth career change*, our *fourth career move*, and our *fourth state move* in the now *thirty-five years of marriage*. So, I know you, ladies, can relate to my hesitancy! But I have to say, in my spirit, I knew it was right if only my flesh could get on board! God had taken Gary and I on a wonderful life journey up to this point, so why rock the boat? I just needed to trust God with our future. Looking back, it seems ridiculous that I had such a hard time with what God was asking of us. Every change and move had been a blessing to our entire family. Now knowing where God took us and why, of course, it makes more sense. I had a lesson to learn. It is in the *unknown* where we learn to trust and depend more on God. Learning to trust God in those unfamiliar places is where our faith grows the most. God alone knows our future and what we will need, and he prepares us for what is coming.

In our walk with God, we are either moving forward and constantly changing from glory to glory more into the likeness of Christ or we are stagnant and not growing. We have the choice of wandering in the wilderness of disobedience or to listen to the voice of the Spirit and be obedient. God wants to change us from one chapter of life to the next. I have found in my life that God never asks me to do easy things that I could manage on my own. But instead, he challenges me to do the things that can only be accomplished by trusting and obeying in him. He wants us to rely on him. God had changed Gary and I in so many ways over the years. Even though we did not always understand at the time. He was preparing us for the greatest challenge and battle we would have to face in this life, a terminal diagnosis of ALS.

## Our Early Years

Gary and I met and fell in love over spring break my senior year of high school. We met in May and were married by September, just six months later! Gary was nineteen and I was eighteen. Looking back, I realize our whirlwind romance and marriage was hard on our parents. We were just babies! After just six months of marriage, Gary got a letter from Uncle Sam saying, "We want you!" He was drafted into the Army and sent to Vietnam just as quickly as we had fell in love. After nearly two years apart, we had to get to know each other all over again. When we got married, I was saved but was not really living for God, and Gary was not saved. For the first twenty-five years of our marriage, Gary had worked at the local electric company. He started out mowing the grass at substations during the summer while a student. Then after we were married, he got on the tree trimming crew. From there, he was promoted to lineman and finally he was promoted to the number two person in the company as the member service director. Oh, and do not let me leave out that we also raised feeder pigs for a brief time! Not something I ever want to do again, but it was a great experience. After Gary came home from Vietnam, we started our family. We had four children over the next eight years. We both attended Berean Bible College and were credentialed as ministers in the Assemblies of God in 1981. We also went on five mission trips to Haiti and Jamaica.

## Drafted and Off to Vietnam

While in Vietnam, Gary's company, the First Cavalry, was part of the invasion into Cambodia. During that invasion, Gary and three other men got separated from their company in the jungle and spent three days and nights in the jungle surrounded by the enemy. Gary prayed during this time and told God that if he would save them, he would serve God for the rest of his life. After they were saved, the men Gary had saved went to the commanding officer and requested Gary be given an award for saving their lives. Gary was honored with the Bronze Star for valor for saving those men, along with several other medals. It took many years of marriage before I found out exactly what he had done to earn that Bronze Star. Whenever asked about the Bronze Star, he always told people that it was for going into Cambodia. He just left out the part where he saved three other men. He never told me the entire story until we had been married over forty years! And it was just like Gary to stay true to his word. In 1972, after coming home from Vietnam, he gave his life to Christ and served God faithfully for the rest of his life!

## A Big Decision

One of the first difficult decisions God asked us to make was to move to Springfield, Missouri. We had lived in Gary's hometown of Marshalltown, Iowa, for twenty-five years and had deep roots there with family, friends, our church family, and career. Gary had been offered a job at an engineering company in Springfield, Missouri. He would be mapping out and designing underground electric grids. God had been dealing with us about full-time ministry but that was and even greater decision. Our oldest daughter, Deanna, was going into her senior year of high school with the same friends she had all her life. She was not happy about the idea of moving, to say the least, and Gary and I certainly understood. We knew the effect our decision would have on our children as well as our extended family. We had decided not to discuss the move with anyone because we wanted to hear from God alone.

The morning we needed to make our final decision, we had our family devotions and then told the kids we were going into our bedroom to pray. When we were done praying, we both had a peace about the choice we decided to make, and we told the kids. Deanna still had an attitude about the move, but we held firm. As we were eating breakfast, there was a knock on our front door. I got up to answer the door and was surprised at who was standing there. It was a friend I did not see often. She went to another church in town where we occasionally would combine efforts with our summer vacation Bible schools. I asked her in, but she said she was on her way to work and could not stay. She seemed rather hesitant but proceeded to tell me that during her devotions that morning, God had spoken to her and asked her to tell Gary and I that *he would be opening a door of opportunity for us and we were to go through that door and not fear or look back!* Wow, was I surprised and shocked. What an awesome confirmation from our loving heavenly Father who understood just how difficult making this decision had been for us. I thanked my friend and let her know that her message was a confirmation of something God had been dealing with us about. I did not share details with her because we had not let our family, church, or Gary's boss know yet. The other beautiful thing that happened was that Deanna had heard this too! She had an "I give up" moment, but she knew it was God!

## First Time as Senior Pastor—
## Rogersville Assembly of God

We were off to Springfield, Missouri, to begin writing the next chapter of our life. We started attending a church that was in our neighborhood, Park Crest Assembly of God. The Church was much larger than we were used to, but it had a great children and youth ministries for our kids. After a while, we found a smaller church outside of Springfield in Rogersville, Missouri, where we felt we could get plugged into and help the pastor. When I say "smaller," I really mean "smaller." It was basically the pastor, his wife, and little girl and our family. We would be offering the pastor instant church growth by attending. The church went from three to nine in one week. Our two older daughters still attended the youth group at Park Crest because the smaller church had nothing for them. Park Crest proved to be such a blessing to our girls as they adjusted to our new life.

Eventually, the pastor at our Rogersville church left to go into the military as a chaplain. He recommended my husband to the district officials to step in as senior pastor. So that was our first full-time ministry. Our first Sunday with Gary as senior pastor, it was only our family. Our son, David, said to Gary, "Guess we can go home since there is nobody here." Gary's response was, "No, we came to worship God, and he's here!" That little church proved to be a real faith builder. One month, we got a fuel bill for the church that was over twelve hundred dollars. We had no idea how we would ever be able to pay the bill since the church had no operating budget. We had taken the church with no salary since we both had other jobs to support our family. The next Sunday, we were excited to have visitors come into the church. It was friends from our church in Iowa. Without a word spoken about our financial dilemma, they put a check in the offering plate. We did not even look at it at first because we were not used to getting any offering. On the drive home that Sunday, I looked at the folded check, and it was for, you guessed it, twelve hundred dollars!

## Church Merge with Mt. Sinai Assembly of God

Eventually, the district decided to merge two churches that were in that same little town, and they asked us to be senior pastors. We received a salary at the next church, nothing you could live on but enough for us to use it to hire a much-needed youth pastor. Now our girls could attend youth at our church. The youth pastor we hired back then now works at Convoy of Hope. Pastor Matt's first Sunday with us was memorable. It was communion Sunday, and two older gentlemen in bib overalls came forward to serve the communion. They got into a very heated discussion at the communion table about how communion was to be served. It seemed that they both had been given instructions by their wives that were not in agreement. Pastor Matt and I were sitting on the front pew and could not look at each other or we would have burst out laughing. That was an interesting little country church.

There was a lady in the congregation who would begin to jiggle her exceptionally large set of keys when it was noon to signal my husband it was time for church to be over. Then there was the man who stood up in the middle of my husband's sermon to inform him that he was only to read from the King James version of the Bible in this church. And there was the time when my daughter, Carrie, and I were in the middle of leading worship when the same man stood up and yelled at us because the chorus we were singing was not out of the hymnal! On another occasion, I was also informed that the puppets I used in children's church were from the devil! We could write a book just about what we learned while pastors at that little country church. But we lived through it and even stayed in ministry!

Our older daughter, Deanna, was in her first year at Evangel College and met her husband-to-be, so we were in the middle of planning their wedding. Gary was working at the engineering company and pastoring the church; I was on staff as children's pastor at yet another church that met only on Sunday nights because they were sharing a building. And I had a day job at Bass Pro in Springfield. Gary's engineering job took him out of town from Monday through Thursday. I am not sure how we did all this, but we quickly decided we needed to do something different.

## Our First Full-Time Position as Senior Pastor— Faith Fellowship Assembly of God

God once again was going to shake our world. After Deanna was married, she and her new husband, Scott, moved to Virginia Beach, Virginia. We took our next family vacation to Virginia to visit our daughter. Before we left on that trip, we had decided to test the waters and send out our résumés to some churches around the country. While we were in Virginia, Deanna and Scott told us of a church that was looking for a pastor in Crisfield, Maryland. When we got home, Gary called the head deacon of the Maryland church and talked to him. He was extremely interested in us because they would be getting two pastors for the price of one. But he told Gary that there was a candidate coming that Sunday and he was certain he would be voted on and hired. He still encouraged Gary to send our résumés because he said, "You never know."

We sent the résumés, and a week later got a call, the candidate missed getting hired by one vote; we were back on our way to the east coast again. The next week, after we got back home, they called and asked us how soon we could be there. That was a whirlwind of decisions, and we were back on the road headed to the eastern shore of Maryland driving the biggest U-Haul truck and trailer we could rent. At the time of this move, our second daughter, Carrie, was in her senior year of high school. This move was a definite culture shock coming from the Midwest, where we had lived all our lives. Gary and I both were on staff and spent seven years at Faith Fellowship in Crisfield, Maryland. We developed a deeper love of the ministry and lifelong friends.

## Move to Gaithersburg, Maryland— Gaithersburg Assembly of God

We were ready to be back in a larger community, and we got our larger community aright! We left small-town living on the eastern shore of Maryland to take a church in Gaithersburg, Maryland, a bedroom community of Washington, DC. This church was a struggling church of about thirty when we got there. It would prove to be a church where God would once again teach us some valuable lessons. The church grew to be about one hundred fifty while we were there. We were also able to help get a Spanish congregation started. The church was multicultural and represented over fifteen countries from around the world. We loved the DC area with all the things to do and its unending possibilities. It was a congregation that was so diverse and in such a large area that it was hard to establish that "family feel" we so longed for. We loved and embraced the diversity. God taught me a valuable lesson there. I learned to be true to myself and who God had designed me to be. I learned to be a "God pleaser" and not a people pleaser. I became much more confident in who I was as a woman, wife, mother, and minister. I also learned to love that congregation and respect who they were. We were there seven years, and I could have stayed longer, but it was at this crossroads where God changed it up once again. He called Gary into the chaplaincy.

## This Boy Is Going Places

Let me tell you about my husband. Gary grew up in rural Iowa on a farm. He was a corn-fed Iowa boy through and through. He always wanted to be a farmer (that is why we raised feeder pigs for a while). But farming in Iowa is not something you get into, you pretty much must be born into it because it is so costly. Gary grew up farming, but his dad was a farmhand, not a farm owner. Gary was an extremely hard worker with outstanding work ethics. He was patriotic and proud of his military service as well as the military heritage we both had. His dad was in the Army during WWII and served in Europe under Patton. My dad served in the Navy aboard the USS Claxton, a Navy destroyer in the Pacific. One of the things I loved about Gary was he always had a good attitude and never spoke unkindly about anyone. He was also the healthiest person I knew. He saw good in people and was never judgmental. He had a way to bring the best out of people and calm to any situation. He was not perfect, but he was the best example of Christ I have ever known. He lived throughout the week what he believed and preached on Sunday.

In our marriage and life, there has not been much downtime. We have always been on the move and enjoyed every adventure. In our marriage of fifty years, we moved twenty-seven times. We have lived in six states and traveled to foreign countries. Gary had four different life careers: the electric co., the engineering co., minister, and chaplain. Early in our first years of marriage, my grandfather once made a comment in passing about Gary, he said, "That boy is going to go places in this life." I did not think much about it at the time, but looking back, I would say it was a prophetic comment!

## Our True Foundation

God established a true foundation early on in our lives because he had work for us to do in his kingdom. We are never through until we take our last breath. Keep on running the race, keep your focus on the prize of heaven. God will open doors of opportunity you never dreamed possible.

Gary was the best example of Christ I have ever known. I am so thankful for having him as my husband for fifty years. I am thankful our children and grandchildren had him as a living example of Christ in their lives. He was not perfect, but he lived out his faith every day. All during his seven-year battle with ALS, he never gave up, and his faith never wavered. He told me in his last days that he was not afraid of death, but he just hated leaving me and the kids. We laughed and cried together, but I assured him that my life with him had been such a blessing, and no woman could feel more loved or cared for than I was. From the diagnosis to his last breath, he was thinking of everyone else, never himself. He was the most selfless person I have ever known.

He had an alarm system put in our house, and I asked him why because we had never had one before. He said because he wanted me to feel safe and I would be living here alone someday. He took out insurance to make sure our home would be paid for when he was gone. He got all his affairs in order and taught me how to pay the bills. He was slowly relinquishing all that he had done for me as the ALS was robbing him of his abilities. He paid the bills until his hands no longer worked. He told me to sell our handicap van and get a new car when he was gone. He even told me that it was okay with him if I wanted to get remarried. I laughed and told him "That ain't happening," he asked why. I told him that he had taken such good care of me and treated me like a queen, and I would never find another man like him. It is the truth. He will always be my forever love. He also asked me what I thought it would be like as a widow. I refused to answer or discuss that with him. I just said that I did not want to think that far ahead. After he was gone, I wished I would have discussed that with him because I think it was his way of preparing me for the future. He was always thinking of others.

As I reflect about being a widow, I do not even like the word "widow." I guess I will get used to it but not right now. I remember the first time I had to fill out a form and mark widow as my marital status, I cried at the very thought. I have discovered that I do not like living by myself. It is so lonely, and I miss Gary so much that my heart hurts. Some days, it is too much, and I give into the grief and have a pity party. Most of the time, God helps me stay strong and put one foot in front of the other and keep moving forward. Gary would want me to continue strong!

God used Gary to help me become the woman I am today. A self-confident, courageous woman of faith. If you have not guessed by now, he was a giver, protector, provider, relaxed, patient, and easy-going type-B personality. On the other hand, I am a type-A personality. We were different in every way, yet we complimented each other perfectly. Together we were stronger, more whole as a couple. He helped me slow down and take life easier, and I would like to think I helped him become the man God wanted him to be. God gave Gary and I a true foundation from the start of our married life, and I intend to live for Christ until my last breath. I will serve others and give God all my praise. It is in him alone I boast!

# CHAPTER 3

## *Thumbs-Up*

Therefore, since we are surrounded by such a cloud of witnesses, let us throw off everything that hinders and the sin that so easily entangles. And let us run with perseverance the race marked out for us, fixing our eyes Jesus, the pioneer and perfecter of faith. For the joy set before him he endured the cross, scorning its shame, and sat down at the right hand of the throne of God. Consider him who endured such opposition from sinners so that you will not grow weary and lose heart.

—Hebrews 12:1–3

## Life Is a Race—The Diagnosis

OUR LIVES ARE a lifelong race and test of our faith. We need to daily get rid of the sin that slows us down and hinders our way to the finish line and our reward of eternal life in heaven. Some of the greatest dangers we face in not finishing strong are our own sins. To win, we must keep our mind, eyes, and heart fixed on Jesus. Part of the challenge is overcoming temptations and suffering. It is a lifelong marathon and learning process that ends only with our last breath!

Life has a way of taking sudden twists and turns that we may not know are coming or be prepared for that can alter our entire future. That happened to our family in June of 2012 with just one short phone call from the Hampton VA Medical Center. I had emailed the director of the hospital about a doctor that had been disrespectful to my husband at his appointment that day. This is after months of testing and worry over what was wrong with my husband and the fear that the diagnosis may be ALS. The doctor had an attitude and acted like our appointment was a bother to him. He said to my husband, "If we can't diagnose you here, you're just out of luck." I had heard enough and got up and walked out of his office in tears. I have never done that before in my life. I also had never contacted an official to complain. That just was not who I am, but I had had enough of this doctor's bad attitude. It was not the first or last time he spoke to my husband like that.

When you are concerned, worried, and fearful of the outcome that takes a year to diagnose, it does not take much to push you over the edge. When we got home, I e-mailed the director of the hospital. Much to my surprise, she immediately returned my call. Nothing at the VA hospital ever happened that fast! I was surprised when I answered the phone, and it was the director. We discussed the doctor visit as she was looking over my husband's medical records. She was apologetic about the doctor, and you could tell that it was not his first complaint. She then mentioned to me that my e-mail had said we still had no diagnosis. We had been to three different VA hospitals, and it had been close to eighteen months of testing and getting second opinions! She then proceeded to tell me that in fact there was a diagnosis in his file confirmed by a second doctor at another VA hospital.

She said, "Mrs. Tingwald, I am sorry to tell you over the phone, but your husband has been diagnosed with Bulbar ALS." It was so unexpected to get the news that way that I was at a loss of what to say. By this time, we were certain what the diagnosis was going to be but still held out hope that we were wrong. Gary was the fourth person in his family to be diagnosed with ALS. There had been someone in the last three generations who had ALS. His cousin was in the final stages at the time Gary was diagnosed. We had seen the devastation of the disease up close and personal.

However, we had never heard of Bulbar ALS. We just thought ALS was ALS. We began right away researching Bulbar ALS only to discover that it was the worst kind—if there can be a worst kind of this horrific disease. Bulbar ALS attacks the muscles of the diaphragm, face, head, and neck. Bulbar ALS usually progresses faster than limb onset ALS. ALS has a life expectancy of 3–5 years. With Bulbar ALS, they give you three years at best. Bulbar ALS is observed in only 30 percent of people with ALS.

## ALS—Amyotrophic Lateral Sclerosis

ALS stands for amyotrophic lateral sclerosis, also known as Lou Gehrig's disease. Lou Gehrig was a famous baseball player who was one of the first to be diagnosed with ALS. ALS is a terminal disease with no cure. It is a disease that affects the nervous system. It weakens the muscles and affects the nerves cells in the brain and spinal cord. Symptoms are loss of coordination, muscle weakness, slurred speech, loss of the ability to speak, muscle cramps, uncontrollable laughter or crying, loss of ability to breathe, swallow, walk, eat, and loss of muscles in the neck so you can no longer hold your head up, excess saliva, and, in a few, frontal lobe dementia. Those are only some of the list of symptoms. Eventually, you are trapped in your body with nothing left but your mind if you do not have dementia.

In Gary's family, each member was affected differently. His cousin had limb onset ALS, which means it affected his arms and legs first. Two of his uncles suffered from frontal lobe dementia. Gary's first symptom was slurred speech. His symptom was so mild it took his sister to bring it to our attention. We were on vacation when she called it to our attention. He was slurring a word now and then but almost undetectable. We thought maybe he had had a mild stroke. So, as soon as we got home from our vacation, he made an appointment with a doctor at the VA hospital in Hampton, Virginia.

I had retired a year earlier with health issues of my own, and we had gone on COBRA Insurance with my former employer. The COBRA Insurance for me was over twelve hundred dollars a month with no prescription coverage, and for the first time in our married life, Gary had no health insurance, so he had signed up at the VA. We were not too worried because he had never had any health problems, and he would be eligible for Medicare in a couple of years. The VA, with all the problems, would turn out to be our saving grace. We began the most difficult journey of our life to find out what was wrong with Gary, never dreaming where it would take us. There is no test for ALS, it is diagnosed by process of elimination. Most people are diagnosed within a year, but Gary's took longer because it was done at the VA. We found out later that he was the first to be diagnosed with ALS at the Hampton, VA medical Center. Most veterans are diagnosed by their civilian primary care physician and then go to the VA for help in procuring all the needed medical supplies and equipment. By the time Gary was diagnosed, we were quite sure of what the diagnosis would be. ALS is a rare disease and even rarer to run in a family. Gary was diagnosed in June of 2012, and he died on February 20, 2018.

## Gary's Unwavering Faith

Gary's faith never wavered, and he always had a good attitude. From day one, Gary had a positive outlook. When we were given his diagnosis, I went all to pieces. Gary, in his calm, mild manner said, "Vickie, we are all terminal, it will be okay." His comment stopped me abruptly in the middle of my pity party. I thought, *If he can stay so calm, then I need to get a grip.* Gary never stopped trusting in his Savior. When friends asked him how he was doing, he would always tell them that his body was wasting away but his spirit was never stronger. That was the truth. Gary taught us all many lessons in trusting God. He will forever be my hero of faith and love of my life.

Toward the end of Gary's illness, I met a lady who recently had been diagnosed with Bulbar ALS and lived in our same condo building. She asked to meet Gary, so I invited her into our home, not thinking about what a shock it would be to her in seeing Gary. Our bedroom was packed with every kind of medical equipment known to man and resembled a hospital room more than a bedroom. We even had a lift on the ceiling that we used to lift Gary into his wheelchair, bathroom, and shower. The look on her face when her husband wheeled her into our bedroom was sheer horror. I immediately knew what was happening because it was the same shock I had felt at going to our first ALS Support Group meeting.

She wanted to go right up to the side of his hospital bed, you knew she had come for a reason. She immediately introduced herself to Gary, then she asked him what she had come to ask, if he had it to do over, would he get the trach? It was an amazing conversation to witness. Neither of them could speak and had to converse with their iPads, but there was an instant bond of understanding. To my surprise, Gary quickly responded, without hesitation, that "no, he would not." He told her it had prolonged his life, but the quality of life was not good. She asked how we had come to our decision. I shared with her our faith, she, too, was a believer, and that we had prayed. We felt God telling us to choose life! Then she asked if it would be a sin to not get a trach. We told her it had to be her own choice and that there was no right or wrong decisions. Then she asked Gary to pray with her. There was not a dry eye in the room. She told us she did not want to live like that, and Gary and I understood completely. Gary even more than the rest of us.

Early on in Gary's diagnosis, we could not understand why most of his doctors did not seem to encourage getting a trach. Looking back, we could understand. They knew firsthand the result and struggles we would face as a family. They told us that there would come a time when we would have to make the harder decision to stop using the trach and turn the vent off. Our friend died within eighteen months of her diagnosis without a trach. There is no right or wrong decisions, only personal choices found in much prayer. The trach prolonged Gary's life, and for that I am thankful for the extra time we had together. He continued to set goals to live for, his last goal was to make it to our fiftieth wedding anniversary. He missed our anniversary by seven months. But he was able to celebrate in heaven, fully healed! The last goal Gary accomplished was to attend our oldest grandson Nathan's high school graduation. We were both in attendance and so enormously proud of Nathan.

Every milestone in my life since then, his absence has been felt. But I rejoice in knowing that I will see him again someday and he will be whole again. I have had a limited view of the sacrifice Jesus made for us on the cross. He died not only for our salvation and healing but for so much more. He died so that we not only could be resurrected like him but so that all his creation would someday be resurrected! He is coming again as our reigning king, and he has promised us a new heaven and a new earth! My goal now is to work while I still can, to store up treasures in heaven, not for myself, but to lay at the feet of my Savior as an offering for all he has done for me!

## The Progression of Gary's ALS

The progression of Gary's ALS seemed to happen rapidly, just like his cousin, Jean, had told us it would. We barely got adjusted to one symptom and found a new normal when another symptom would start. His first symptom had been slurred speech. He rapidly lost strength in his diaphragm, causing trouble in his breathing and volume of speech. Dealing with ALS, you learn way more about the human body than you ever wanted to know. Gary was still active in the chaplaincy ministry, but his speech had become a problem. He was not only getting harder to understand but also because his diaphragm was being affected, he did not have enough breath for volume. In the jail setting, it is loud and you need to be able to speak loudly.

The VA equipped him with a voice amplifier that he could wear around his waist like a fanny pack. It was simply a microphone for his voice. Gary was respected by the inmates, and someone would always yell "Chaplain on the floor" when he arrived. That was more for the swearing to stop than anything, but after Gary needed the voice amplifier, they even got a little quieter for him. The jail where he was chaplain had no chapel, so you had to minister through the bars at each overcrowded cell. Gary saw it as an advantage (his positive nature again) because he said that the guys who really wanted no part of it still had to listen!

His next challenge was fatigue. He had to go to half days in his office and give up going into the jail. He was the senior chaplain, which I will talk more about later, over twenty plus facilities and 8,000 inmates in the Hampton Rhoads area. Eventually, even the half days became too much, so he had to "retire," a word we never used. Gary and I had planned to be active in ministry as long as we were able. But God often has different plans for us. Gary loved ministry and especially the men and women he ministered to, so this was a hard pill to swallow, but he knew it was time. He was still walking and talking, but each day was becoming more difficult for him.

## Veterans Administration ALS Clinic

The next chapter of our lives was harder yet. We had to sell our home and downsize. We lived in a 2,000-square-foot home on a golf course that we both loved. The problem was the upkeep on the house and the big yard. We knew we would not be able to manage it all in the future. The house was an older home built in the 1950s with tiny bathrooms, narrow hallways, and small bedrooms. That was not going to work for a wheelchair or Gary's care. We sold our home and moved into an apartment near our daughter until we could figure out our next move. That would mean two moves in one year while dealing with a terminal illness.

By this time, Gary was in leg braces and using a cane. This stage only lasted a brief time. He soon had to start using a walker. After Gary's cousin, Tim, died from his ALS battle, his wife gave us the best advice. She said to try and stay ahead of the disease because it progresses so fast. She told us that they were in the process of remodeling their bathroom to accommodate her husband's wheelchair when he died. She had been taking him to the YMCA twice a week to bathe him.

We found a condo building under construction that had first floor units that would work for us, so we began a construction project with the VA as our ADA contractor. The housing contractor worked so well with the VA, that was a blessing with all we were dealing with.

We applied for a VA construction grant and got approved. That meant that all the ADA adaptations we had to make would be paid for by the VA. After the construction was completed, the VA Grant paid down a portion of our home loan. Another miracle and blessing.

We also found out that as a 100 percent disabled veteran, Gary qualified for the property tax exemption. That meant that as long as we live in this condo, we do not have to pay property taxes. We were made aware of all these benefits when we attended the ALS Clinic at the Washington, DC, VA hospital. If you are a veteran with ALS, I encourage you to attend this clinic!

Let me take a moment to talk about the VA ALS Clinic because it was life changing for our family. Each month, the VA hospital in Washington, DC, holds an ALS Clinic. You go to an individual room like a doctor's office, and a whole battery of doctors who specialize in ALS come in, one at a time, to examine Gary and talk to us. One of our daughters always went with us to take notes so we would remember everything. After you have seen all the doctors, a veterans benefit representative comes in to talk to you about your VA benefits. He will tell you about new benefits each month as you become eligible. That is where we found out about the grant programs the VA offers. They have grants for handicap vehicles, grants to remodel your existing home and make it ADA approved, grants to build a new house and even reduced rate mortgage insurance for veterans. Plus, as a 100-percent disabled veteran, you receive a monthly awarded amount from the VA. Your spouse continues to get a set amount after the veteran dies. And by attending the clinic, we found out about the property tax exemption as well as reduced cost license plates for our car. My sister-in-law's husband was 100 percent disabled for years, but they never knew about the property tax exemption until Gary got sick. For years, they had paid property taxes they did not need to be paying. She knows now!

But here is the greatest benefit, besides the veterans benefit representative, you also see a psychologist. At our first clinic, Gary had just recently been diagnosed, so we were still trying to wrap our minds around his terminal diagnosis when they send in the psychologist! She begins to talk about "end of life" preparations, and immediately it felt like the room was closing in on me, and I had such an urge to run out of the room. You have been in that small room now for over four hours and your mind is reeling with all the doctor information, along with being newly diagnosed, and the last thing you want to discuss with a total stranger is the imminent death of your husband! But let me tell you, I am so thankful for that time each month. She would ask us what we had taken care of since seeing her last, and we would go another round of "end of life" talks! We quickly realized, however, that even though it was difficult to have that subject in your face each month, it made it increasingly easier for Gary and I to discuss it together when we were alone.

After Gary passed away, a friend, whose husband had been diagnosed the same time as Gary and had passed before Gary, came to me and asked me, "Why are you doing so much better with your grief than I am?" I felt I knew the answer but hesitated to tell her. They had not had the benefit of attending the ALS Clinic in DC, and I knew that the clinic and my faith is what made the difference. Before Gary died, we were able to discuss every detail of what and how he wanted things done. And because of that, nothing had been left unsaid between us. Gary died while in hospice care and at his choice to stop using the vent. Death is not easy, but the more you are prepared, it helps ease your loss. Gary and I had discussed every detail, and all the plans were made before he passed. Everything you can do to prepare helps. It does not make it easy, but it does help to feel like you have said all you needed to say.

## Who Are We and Where Did Our Life Go?

Our life was changing rapidly. We no longer even resembled our former selves in so many ways. We were both retired now, which we never expected or planned for and certainly not at age sixty-three. Because we were both ministers, we had never planned to retire. We just wanted to change our style of ministry after social security age. We had planned on traveling and helping struggling churches and pastors around our country. Our denomination has a program for older pastors called the Maps Program. You travel around the US and help in any way you can from preaching, building, VBS, to just encouraging a pastor. It is a way to use your talents and time to continue working for the Lord. But we soon realized that God had other plans. We knew we did not want our lives to be filled with sorrow and self-pity. We sat down and talked about what we wanted our home, family, and lives to look like during this time. We decided that we had two choices in dealing with our circumstance. We could hang our heads and feel sorry for ourselves or continue to have our home filled with love, laughter, and joy!

Our choice was to continue to have our lives reflect Christ. When people came into our home, we wanted them to feel the love and presence of God, not sorrow. We made the choice to enjoy our life for as long as possible. We began by planning a trip. We wanted to travel for as long as Gary's health would allow. We went to Anna Maria Island, Florida, for a month. My brother let us use his condo there. Then we went to the Midwest and to Disney with my sister. Our last trip was to the Biltmore Estates in North Carolina. We knew that would be our last trip. It was sad to think about, but we just felt blessed to have gotten to do some traveling.

## Gary's "Thumbs-Up" Attitude

During Gary's illness and to this very day, our home is always filled with praise. Praise to our precious Lord and Savior. Praise in music and in word! Gary wanted to go on living with a purpose and focus on our Savior. Every visitor to our home remembers his "thumbs-up" attitude. Whenever you asked him how he was doing, he would always give you a thumbs-up no matter how bad his day was. He had days with a lot of pain on top of everything else. I would call our children and ask them to pray for him. Deanna, our oldest daughter, would often stop by, especially if she knew he was having a bad day. On one such day, she went into his room concerned and asked him how he was doing. He gave her a smile and a thumbs-up! After she left, I asked him why he did that when I knew how much pain he was suffering. He typed on his iPad, "It is my way of a positive confession!" That day, I loved him even more.

After Gary died, Deanna brought me a gift from a friend at our church. She had peeked in the bag, and she said that she thought it was a gag gift! As soon as I pulled it out of the bag and unwrapped the tissue paper, I knew it was not a gag gift and I started crying. It was a 15-inch-high ceramic "Thumbs-Up" statue! It proudly stands on a shelf in my living room, displayed for all to see as a reminder of Gary's faith and trust in God. By God's immeasurable grace and by the power of the Holy Spirit living in him, Gary kept his thumbs-up attitude until his last breath! His love and example of faith has made me a better person.

## Blessed by Every Provision

By now, we had moved into our new condo that was fully equipped for Gary and his wheelchair. When we moved in, he was still walking with his walker. He began to take some falls, and we knew that his legs were getting weaker. He no longer was able to speak, he was unable to swallow, so he had to have a feeding tube put into his stomach. He took all his food (liquid) and medications through the feeding tube. He also had a trach put in to help him breathe. He would get on the vent at night to rest his lung. Eventually, he had to be on the vent continually. He was still able to use his hands, which was such a blessing. Most ALS patients lose the use of their hands early on, but Gary was fortunate because he could communicate by typing on his iPad. He had been fitted by the VA with a neurotransmitter talking program but never had to use it. He had the use of his hands up until the last few months of his life.

Because he was falling, I told him that we needed to retire the walker. He talked me into letting him use it just a little while longer. But one day, he fell in the living room. and I could not get him up. I asked him that if I got him to the bedroom, could he help me get him up using the cedar chest. He indicated that he could. Our condo had laminate wood floors to accommodate his wheelchair, and they were slippery. I began dragging him into the bedroom, but I had to stop once in a while because we were both laughing so hard at what we must look like. It was funny but at the same time serious because he could have been hurt. That was the last time he used the walker. He had to use his wheelchair from then on. With every new symptom, we would grieve the loss and move on to the next. With ALS, the symptoms happen suddenly, without warning.

One day he was struggling to talk, and the next day he could not talk because it was just too hard. With every new symptom, there was a loss of some bodily function. With each loss, his care became harder for me. He was bothered more by that than I was. He hated me having to do so much for him. He was a caregiver at heart and always took such good care of me. I came to treasure my time with him. I realized that God had prepared me for such a time as this. To care for him became my greatest calling. I had many health issues and was surprised at how God helped me during those days. My biggest frustration was not having the strength and stamina at times that it took. I am so thankful that God allowed and enabled me to care for Gary.

Gary was able to use his hands until the last few months of his life. It got progressively harder for him, and eventually, like every other loss, it just got too hard, and he stopped communicating except with a few hand signals we had devised over the years. That was the turning point for him. He was now in constant pain from bed sores and was down to about 75 or 80 pounds. His healthy weight had been around 170 pounds. He was literally just skin and bones. One morning, while I was taking care of him, he indicated to me that it was time. And I knew what he was referring to. He let me know that he wanted the vent turned off. I embraced him, and we both cried, but I understood and respected his decision. It was that difficult decision the doctors had warned us about. Gary and I discussed this decision long before the time came to make it. Promises were made that we would both be strong. So, here we were at the crossroads I had dreaded.

I spoke to the hospice nurse when she came that morning. She explained everything to me before she went into see Gary. But before she spoke to him, she told me that when the vent is turned off, we would stop feeding him also. Immediately, I told her no, I could not and would not do that. She asked if she could speak to Gary and ask him. I agreed, and we went into talk to him. He very readily agreed that would be fine. It still took me a few days and for his hospice caregiver to tell on me to the nurse before I could stop his food. She explained to me that it would make his passing easier and quicker. Gary held on for thirty-seven days! Those were the most agonizing and painful days of my life. He was asleep most of the time. I would sit for hours and hold his hand and get into his hospital bed with him and just hold him. There is nothing more painful than watching the one you love die a slow death while all you can do is stand by and can do nothing.

## The Goodness of God

During those last weeks, we had lots of company. Our children took turns and made sure that there was always someone with us. We all sat in the bedroom with Gary because that is what he loved, his family all around him. He slept, but we always assumed he could hear us. During that time, there were a few occasions where we thought he had passed because of his breathing, and we all cried and then he would rally. We had all told him that it was all right for him to go. It got to be kind of funny because everyone who came would ask us if we had told him we would be all right and he could go. I am sure he was tired of us giving him permission to leave us!

After Gary died, someone asked me if it bothered me that Gary died at home. I said, "No, because Jesus and the angels were in my home." That bedroom is where I spend most of my time and write this book from that very same room.

The night before Gary died, a friend and chaplain came by and asked if it was all right for her to pray for Gary's healing. We had never given up hope for God to heal Gary, and we agreed by faith for her to pray. Like the three Hebrew children told the King Nebuchadnezzar, in the book of Daniel. "King Nebuchadnezzar, we do not need to defend ourselves before you in this matter. If we are thrown into the blazing furnace, the God we serve is able to deliver us from it, and he will deliver us from Your Majesty's hand. But even if he does not, we want you to know, Your Majesty, that we will not serve your gods or worship the image of gold you have set up" (Daniel 3:17–18).

Like Shadrach, Meshach, and Abednego, we knew God was able. He took Gary home to be with him the next morning. God does not always answer our prayers in the way we ask or think they should be at times. Because God knows all our tomorrows; he also knows what we need and what is best for us. The goodness of God is found in his perfect love for us. The Word of God tells us that all good and perfect gifts come from God. Whenever God answers our prayers, he answers them out of his goodness and love. He will always answer them in a way that is for our best. You may still be asking why Gary never got healed, but you see, I believed God did answer our prayers that night. He healed Gary by taking him home to heaven. Like Gary said to me, "We are all terminal." Whether we are healed in this life or not, we all still will face death.

## God Is Faithful

That same night, Gary started labored breathing. Melissa, our youngest daughter, and I sat with him for a couple hours, and his breathing got better, so I told Melissa to go on back to bed. I got in bed with Gary and held him for a couple more hours, and at around 6:30 a.m., I went to my bed next to him. The next morning around 8:00 a.m., I woke to Melissa sitting by Gary's bedside. She said to me, "I think Dad is gone." I checked him and could tell by looking at him that he was gone. The strange thing is that neither one of us broke down and cried. I think we were all cried out, and it was a relief to see Gary out of pain, his battle with ALS was finally over. He had run his best race and now could receive his rewards. I am certain that he heard God say, "Well done, good and faithful servant!"

God has taught me that through all the trials and suffering of the past seven years, that caring for Gary was the highest calling and greatest blessing of my life. Gary had been easy to love and care for because of his positive "thumbs-up" attitude through it all. It had always been difficult for Gary that I had to take care of him. But I was always quick to remind him that not only did I know he would do the same for me but that the vows we had said fifty years ago were "in sickness and in health."

# CHAPTER 4

## *Life-Changing Lessons*

And the God of all grace, who has called you to
his eternal glory in Christ after you have suffered
a little while, will himself restore you and make
you strong, firm, and steadfast.

—1 Peter 5:10

### Life Lesson: Refined by Fire

OVER THE LAST seven years of suffering with the difficulties of a
terminal illness, God has taught our family many life-changing lessons. In these lessons, we have grown spiritually, and we have become
even more determined in running the race God has called us to run.
These lessons have helped us to find the "joy in the journey." We are
all being refined by the fire of God's amazing grace each day!

When you hear about ALS and that it is such a horrible disease,
you cannot imagine any good associated with this terminal diagnosis.
It all depends on the condition of our heart and the perception of the
mind. For our family, we have lived the nightmare called ALS. We
could begin by listing all the terrible symptoms because we witnessed
ALS up close and personal, taking the life of my husband little by

little. But instead, let me share with you the powerful lessons we have learned. We saw Gary, who was to us a husband, a father, a grand-father, and a brother, and so much more, fight this disease daily. And what we saw was a man of God who never wavered in his faith. He handled every new symptom with faith and grace. When he was asked how he was doing, he always answered like this, "My body is failing but my spirit is strong!" It was with that positive attitude that he faced each new day with every new challenge. I would like to tell you how God turned our difficult ALS journey into something good and life-changing.

## Life Lesson: New Priorities

Facing a terminal illness will change your priorities quickly. Things that were important before the diagnosis quickly lose their importance. The wood, straw, and stubble of our lives are the unim-portant things that really do not make a difference in eternity. Those things are suddenly stripped away, and you are left with a completely different value system. You are aware of how the real and true trea-sures of life have eternal value. Before your difficulty, you treasured so many things with no eternal value whatsoever. Treasures like your home, your car, your position or career, your bank account, your standing in the community, to list just a few. There are many more I could list, but you get the picture.

"Do not store up for yourselves treasures on earth, where moth and rust destroy and where thieves break in and steal. But store up for yourselves treasures in heaven, where moth and rust do not destroy and where thieves do not break in and steal. For where your treasure is, there your heart will be also" (Matthew 6: 19–21).

Gary and I had always talked about how healthy he was, but did we count it as a blessing? I, on the other hand, had many health issues, but did we praise God for all the good reports over the years? We worked hard in the ministry and valued the opportunities God had given us, but did we see it as a treasure we were storing up in heaven? I can truthfully answer yes to these questions, but after Gary's diagnosis, these treasures took on an even deeper meaning in our life.

As ALS continued to rob Gary of his bodily functions we had taken for granted, we were more keenly aware of how much God blesses us each day when our bodies function as he had designed them to function. The simple things we often take for granted. When we wake up in the morning, that means God has given us another day of life to make investments. Invest wisely, invest in the eternal treasures that are stored in heaven where the Bible says they cannot be destroyed. When we invest only in earthly things, they can easily be destroyed. And like the old saying goes, "You can't take them with you." What you should invest in are the things that are near to the heart of God. Today, try investing in his eternal kingdom by telling others about all he has done for you. Be obedient to God's will for your life, he will never fail you. Never boast in yourself, instead boast in Christ and make him famous!

## Life Lesson: Planning for the Unknown

A terminal illness will cause you to look ahead and plan for an unknown future by trusting more in Father God. Doctors can give you a terminal diagnosis, but only God knows when we will take our last breath. After Gary was diagnosed, we were surprised by the number of friends who passed away during Gary's battle with ALS. We understood that life is uncertain at best, and we never can know the outcome. But I believe that God wants us to prepare in many ways. You can prepare emotionally, physically, spiritually, and financially. Always trusting that it is God alone who has the perfect plan for your life.

## Lesson Learned: God's Presence

Living with a terminal illness draws you closer than you have ever been to God and one another. There was a sense of God's presence in our home and life like we had never known. We had prayed and asked God to fill our home with his presence and joy. We wanted to go on living, loving, and laughing. And God showed himself strong in the peace and joy that filled our home. Everyone that came to visit remarked about the presence of God they felt. Even our hospice team laughed about how they would argue about who got to go to the Tingwalds. That was exactly how we had prayed for it to be. On our most difficult days, we would play nonstop praise music and worship God. You will never feel closer to God than when your life depends on him just to get out of bed each day and face the unknown challenges that are waiting for you.

Many who have experienced great suffering would tell you that it was at those times when they felt the greatest presence of God. I can tell you from our experience that it is true. During Gary's illness, we both felt such a strong presence of God. And now, I still feel God's divine presence, but I believe his presence is felt more in our times of need, not because God's presence has changed, but we draw closer to him at those times. We can always know God's presence in our lives. You will have an overwhelming peace and sense of victory. Our trials in life are where we defeat the enemy and where our testimony comes from. We can have joy in the journey even in our darkest hour, knowing that God is always right there beside us, raising our arms in the battle!

## Lesson Learned: Saying Our Goodbyes

ALS afforded us the time to say our goodbyes. Many never get that opportunity when their life is suddenly cut short. Gary and I took the quiet moments alone to talk about our life together, all the blessings God had given us, and how if we had it to do over, we both would! We shared how much we loved one another and said the things that we did not always take the time to say. I wanted Gary to know how happy my life had been because of him. I wanted him to know how much I admired, loved, and saw him as my hero. I wanted him to know that I felt he was the best husband and dad I could have ever asked or prayed for! And I wanted him to know that I was a better person for having him in my life. We talked about how we met and our brief time of dating. I told him that I would never recommend to anyone that they marry after only knowing each other for six months but that I was glad we did because it gave us just that much more time together. We talked about our children and grandchildren. We discussed our hopes and dreams for them and how blessed we were to have such a great family. We both knew that we were not perfect, but we were blessed by God's grace and love.

Gary wanted to talk about what I thought my life would be like when he was gone. I never wanted to discuss that because I did not want to even think about that time to come. I could only handle this journey one day at a time. Looking back, I wish I had discussed that more with him. For his comfort and mine. I would love some of his wisdom now. But it was just too hard to wrap my mind around him not being in my life. Never be afraid to talk about anything with your loved ones, it will enrich your lives. Because we discussed everything, I never felt like I was second guessing what or how he would have wanted things done. It gave me great peace of mind. And when the time came and the decisions had already been made, I could just relax in the love and comfort of my family. We left nothing unsaid, and as we looked at our life together, we realized just how blessed we were.

## Lesson Learned: Love Like There Is No Tomorrow

Because of ALS, we loved like there was no tomorrow. We had always been a couple to show affection, but ALS made us step it up even more. When Gary could not speak, he would type on his iPad "I love you." It always melted my heart. Then when that became hard for him to type, he learned to sign I love you. We signed that to each other all day long. We would lay in his hospital bed and hold one another. On the night he passed away, I got in bed with him and just held him. He could no longer respond to me, but I wanted him to feel the comfort and peace of being held in my arms. I am so glad I did that. To know that he was being held at that moment gives me such joy and peace, even now in my grief. The time you're given never seems like enough. You want one more day. One more time to say I love you. One more chance to tell your loved one just how much they have meant to you. So, never waste a minute that you are given.

# Lesson Learned: Our Hope Never Changes

We learned that our hope does not change because of our circumstances. No matter what difficulty we are facing, we can always know that Jesus will always be our hope. If we keep our focus on Jesus, he will be our hope and stay. The song "In Christ Alone" is my life song and says it all perfectly!

In Christ Alone

In Christ alone my hope is found
He is my light, my strength, my song
The cornerstone, this solid ground
Firm through the fiercest drought and storm
What heights of love, what depths of peace?
When fears are stilled, when thriving cease
My comforter, my all in all
Here in the love of Christ I stand

\* \* \*

In Christ alone who took on flesh
Fullness of God in helpless babe
The gift of love and righteousness
Scorned by the ones he came to save
Till on that cross as Jesus died
The wrath of God was satisfied
For every sin on him was laid
Here in the death of Christ I live

\* \* \*

There in the ground his body lay
Light of the world by darkness slain
Then bursting forth in glorious day
Up from the grave he rose again

And as he stands in victory
Sin's curse has lost its grip on me
For I am his and he is mine
Bought with the precious blood of Jesus Christ

\* \* \*

No guilt in life, no fear in death
This is the power of Christ in me
From life's first cry to final breath
Jesus commands my destiny
No power of hell, no scheme of man
Can ever pluck me from his hand
Till he returns or calls me home
Here in the power of Christ I will stand

## Lesson Learned: The Fiery Furnace of ALS

In Christ alone I will stand! Our family was thrown into the fiery furnace of ALS, but even in the fire, we found Christ to be faithful. In that fire, we found that we could stand and come out unharmed by Satan's schemes. In that fire, we realized we were never alone. In the fire, we were tested, and by God's amazing grace, our faith was refined and became even stronger! God did not deliver us from ALS. God did not change our circumstance, but he was always right there in the flames with us. The flames of ALS helped to make us stronger and more determined to follow Christ because we discovered the power of Christ in us to be overcomers! None of us want to go through the fire, but it is in the furnace where we take our stand. It was the test of the fiery furnace where the three Hebrew children made their stand of faith in their God. No matter what, they told the king they trusted their God no matter the outcome. ALS was the fire of our testing, and it was in that testing that we learned to trust and hang on to God's hand as he stood with us and gave us the strength to face the fire!

"In this you greatly rejoice, though now for a little while you may have had to suffer grief in all kinds of trials. These have come so that your faith—of greater worth than gold, which perishes even though refined by fire—may be proved genuine and may result in praise, glory, and honor when Jesus Christ is revealed" (1 Peter 1: 6–7).

"See, I have refined you, though not as silver; I have tested you in the furnace of affliction" (Isaiah 48:10).

Often God will test our faith. You might think that just does not sound right. Let me point you to his word and truth. The refiner's fire is found all through God's word. You can find it in the scriptures listed above, but let me give you some more to think about: Zechariah 13:9, Malachi 3:3, Malachi 3:1–18, Job 23:10, Proverbs 17:3, Psalm 66:10–12, 1 Peter 4:12–13, just to list a few, there are many more. We are told several times to rejoice in the testing! That really does not sound right, but we can rejoice when we make it through the test and come out stronger in our faith. The test not only shows God where we are in our faith walk, but it also shows us when we experience the victory over suffering; we are encouraged and stronger in our resolve and faith. Each time we have a victory, large or small, our faith grows stronger. Some tests are more difficult than others, but all serve a purpose in God's greater plan for our lives. God knows what we will face in our future, and he uses the tests to prepare and strengthen us to be ready for the challenge!

## Lesson Learned: God Is Sovereign

It is through the testing that we become more secure in our faith. Even when we think we have done a lot for God and have been faithful, we still do not get a "get out of suffering" card. It also does not mean we will get every prayer answered the way, when, and how we want. God is sovereign, and we need to love and trust him even when he does not answer our prayers how and when we think he should. Who are we to think we have done so much for God? God does not need our help to run the universe. He calls us to be obedient and follow and trust him. He tells us that obedience is better than sacrifice. We should always serve God out of a heart of love and obedience. We are to always be mindful that God is a good Father and the giver of good gifts. He knows what we need and when we will need it. We must put our trust in him as our provider. He will never leave you alone. He is always right beside us in the fire!

## Lesson Learned: God Will Use Our Brokenness

Our suffering and brokenness do not mean we are unusable. God loves us and will use our brokenness for his glory. It is in that brokenness that we become stronger and grow in our faith. When we are broken and humbled by the trials of life, we realize just how much we need God. God will take all the broken pieces of our life and give us a testimony that will touch hearts for his kingdom and give him glory. I am reminded of the potter and the clay illustration in the Bible. Our lives are the clay in God's almighty and strong hands, he is the potter. The potter can mold and reshape the clay into a beautiful and useful vessel. All we need to do is trust the hands of the potter. "'O house of Israel, can I not do with you what the potter does?' declares the Lord. 'Like clay in the hand of the potter, so are you in my hand, O house of Israel'" (Jeremiah 18:6).

The clay does not get to choose what it wants to be, the use and design of the vessel is in the hands of the potter. If there is a flaw in the vessel, the potter can reshape and mold the clay into something useful and beautiful. God can take the broken pieces of our lives and give them purpose and meaning that will glorify him! God can use times of suffering to shape us into a vessel of honor. A vessel worthy of giving God all the glory!

## Lesson Learned: Rejoice in Our Suffering

ALS helped us understand why God calls us to suffer and how to know his joy and peace in the middle of our circumstance. When we look at God's Word, we can hardly turn a page without reading about suffering. We so often miss the suffering scriptures in our search for the benefits and promises. But God makes it more than clear in his word that we all *will* suffer. From the moment we ask Christ into our lives, Satan has a target on our backs! If we are living for Christ, the enemy will be prowling like a lion, looking for ways to destroy us. In the conflict and struggle, God tells us to rejoice. Our human nature computes that as a contradiction, but in God's kingdom, many things are the opposite of how the world sees them.

"And we rejoice in the hope of the glory of God. Not only so, but we also rejoice in our sufferings because we know that suffering produces perseverance, perseverance character, and character hope, and hope does not disappoint us because God has poured out his love into our hearts by the Holy Spirit whom he has given us" (Romans 5:3–5).

## Lesson Learned: Opportunities from ALS

ALS gave us the opportunity to minister and witness to people we would never have meant otherwise. Doctors, nurses, hospice workers, caregivers, therapists, and our ALS family and friends. ALS helped us to see how beautiful it can be when all we have left is our faith, trust, and hope in God. ALS taught us how strong we are in our faith, as well as where we are weak and need to grow. It is funny because people would tell me how strong I was because of all I had to do to care for Gary. But the truth was that I did not feel strong, in fact, most of the time I was so fearful of all the new responsibilities. There were times when I was not sure I could get through another hour. ALS caused me to lean on and trust in God so I could dig deeper and do more than I thought physically, emotionally, and spiritually possible. The Bible tells us that when we are at our weakest, God will make us strong, believe it, it is true!

## Lesson Learned: Mysteries of God's Word

ALS kept us seeking and searching God's Word for understanding, and somewhere along the journey, the word came alive like never before. It is interesting how much more you get out of the Word of God when you are reading it with your life depending on it and not just casually reading it as a devotion. We should always read the Word of God as if our life depended on it because it does. Every day we are in a spiritual battle for our life, and we need God's Word to lead us, guide us, protect us, challenge us, save us, teach us, and show us the narrow way to our goal, heaven. God's word will have deeper meaning each time we read it as we are growing and maturing spiritually. In our Christian walk, we are either growing or standing still. If we are standing still, we are not going anywhere but most likely losing ground. We need to be changing and growing more into the likeness of Christ every day.

## Lesson Learned: Forgiveness

ALS taught us to forgive because life is too short to hold on to unforgiveness. And ALS reminded us that Christ has suffered everything we will ever suffer. He knows and understands our pain and suffering like none other. Christ forgave while he hung on the cruel cross of Calvary. He forgave those who had beaten him, those who had despised and mocked him, those who had spit on him, the men who drove the nails in his hands and feet, the spiritual leaders who did not recognize him as the Messiah, Peter who had denied him three times, those hanging beside him, and all of humanity that would sin and need a Savior. On that cross, Christ looked down through time and saw you and me, and he willingly died to forgive all our sins. If he could forgive all that, should we not forgive even more generously? He made a deposit of forgiveness in our account in heaven. Have you freely offered forgiveness from your account? He chose to forgive us while suffering the agony of the cross, so no matter what pain or suffering we experience, he is our example of how to forgive.

While Gary was enduring each day of losing his bodily functions, he was never cross or angry with anyone. How he suffered spoke so loudly to those of us who were with him every day. It made you stop and think about how you would react given that same circumstances. When you frequent ALS caregiver websites, you read about how so many people who are suffering take out their frustrations and anger on their caregiver. That is probably more of the average reaction. None of us know how we would cope. It also makes you think about just how much Jesus suffered for us and still responded with love to the very ones crucifying him. That is the unconditional love of our Savior.

## Lesson Learned: Seeing in the Dark

ALS helped us to realize that we can still see with our eyes of faith in our darkest hours. God's love and care for us shines the brightest at those times to show us the way. He is the lamp unto our feet and a light to keep us on the right path. There were days when we felt like we were stumbling around in the dark, not knowing which way to turn. But we discovered that God was always there to lead and guide us. God gave us strength and courage to face another day as we struggled with the "unknown." With ALS, we faced the unknown every day. Gary would never know what new symptom he would face each day when he woke up. And when the symptoms came, we had to figure out how to adjust our lives to the new normal. We had to come up with the best medical care for the problem and how we would implement that care. In those difficult times, we could always turn to God for our peace and comfort. He was faithful to always guide us and show us the way.

## Lesson Learned: God Is in the Battle

ALS taught us that God may not take us out of the battle, but he is always right there with us, even fighting the battle for us. We had to learn to let go and let him do the heavy lifting when we had nothing left to give. There were times when we were surrounded by fear and uncertainty, but God was always there with us in the battle.

Psalm 24:8 says this, "Who is the king of glory? The Lord strong and mighty, the Lord mighty in battle."

Christ fought and won every battle for us at Calvary! We are already the victors! We just need to get our flesh and spirit lined up with God's Word. We all need an Aaron and Hur to hold up our hands in the middle of the battle when we grow weak. You can read that story in the book of Exodus 17:6–16. While in battle with the Amalekites, as Moses held up his staff, the Israelites were winning. But when he got tired and lowered his hands, they began to lose the battle. When Aaron and Hur saw this, they went to Moses and help hold his hands up to keep the staff raised. We all need someone we can trust, to be our "caregiver" when we become too tired and weary in the battles of life. I was Gary's caregiver, but I had many caregivers myself. My family, my church, the ALS community, hospice, and many doctors. No one can stand alone. My greatest caregiver was the Lord Jesus himself. He gave me strength and courage to stay in the battle!

## Lesson Learned: When We Are Weak, Jesus Makes Us Strong

ALS helped us to understand that even at our weakest moments, we are victorious in Christ. We need to keep running in the race and stay focused on Christ. We must always run our best race. To run our best race, we need to train by reading God's Word. We need to always listen to the voice of God and not be distracted by all the other noise around us. We must remember that we need to run the race that God has laid out before us. God's word tells us to run with perseverance the race he has marked out for us.

"Therefore, since we are surrounded by such a cloud of witnesses, let us throw off everything that hinders and the sin that so easily entangles. And let us run with perseverance the race marked out for us, fixing our eyes on Jesus, the pioneer and perfecter of faith. For the joy set before him, he endured the cross, scorning its shame, and sat down at the right hand of the throne of God" (Hebrews 12:1–2).

Jesus was able to endure the cross because he kept his focus on the prize. The prize was his great joy in the salvation on mankind. We should follow his example and always keep our eyes on the prize. Our prize is eternity spent in the presence of God and fellowship with

Christ. God loves us, and he is our greatest cheerleader. Just knowing that Jesus desires to be with us should keep us going!

I will never forget the sermon given at Gary's Mom's funeral. The pastor basically told us that her life's race was over, and she was now passing the baton on to us and we were to run our best race. It was an amazing challenge for us all to live up to. Gary ran his best race, and now it is up to us to take the baton and *run our best race.*

## Lesson Learned: God Writes Our Life Story

ALS taught us that God may write our life story different than we had planned, but we learned to trust that God was writing our story with a much bigger and better plot than we could ever understand. That story includes our eternal life and the way we will get there. The story also has many unexpected twists in the plot. When things do not go as we had planned, we tend to become frustrated and even disappointed, maybe even angry. Gary and I had our retirement years all planned out. But God had different plans. Gary handled the changes much better than I did. I was angry for a time and then disappointed. Gary's steadfast faith helped me to come to terms with what life had dealt us and even accept the peace of God. We never gave up hope for him to get healed but had to also face the possibility that God had us on a completely different course than we would have ever chosen. Then began the process of accepting God's will and trying to figure the lessons he wanted us to learn and to accept the grace to continue in faith.

## Lesson Learned: People Want to Fix You

ALS taught us that well-meaning people often wanted to "fix us" even though God did not see us as broken. They could not understand or accept that ALS just might be God's plan for our lives. Gary's ALS was not caused by God, but God permitted the ALS for his plan and his purpose. A purpose we may never understand. ALS taught us that God sometimes takes us down a road we had never planned on, but we learned to follow because his way is always the best.

In John 9 where Jesus heals the blind man, he first sets the disciples straight by telling them that his blindness was not caused by the sin of he or his parents. Jesus told them that *it happened so his Father God could be glorified.* That was the purpose of the affliction. Then Jesus spit, using his very own DNA, in the dirt from where we were created and rubbed the mud on the blind man's eyes. Then he told the man to go and wash his eyes in the pool of Siloam. The man did as Jesus had instructed and washed his eyes and came back seeing! When the man went home, his relatives, friends, and neighbors doubted that he was the blind man they knew. The blind man himself told them that he was their friend and relative, and he gave God the glory for his healing. It is amazing how people work hard at not believing miracles. They seem to have a need to explain God right out of the event.

It always surprises me that we can believe the negative so much more than we can trust the truth of a miracle. Our human nature only wants to believe the worst while, as Christians, we should be shouting the victory and glorifying God. Gary and I had Christian friends that asked if there was sin in Gary's life causing his ALS. We had people question our faith in God's healing power. Gary and I never gave up or stopped believing that God could heal him at any moment. But God chose not to heal him in the way others thought he should be healed. We believed it was so the Father would be glorified somehow.

There are some questions that we will never have answered in this life. It is our response to the test of our faith that is important. Do we go on believing and trusting or do we just walk away from God? So many choose to walk away from their faith at those crossroads. Gary and I and our family choose to walk by faith and keep on keeping on with God. Like the three Hebrew children who told King Nebuchadnezzar, in Daniel 3:17–18, "If we are thrown into the blazing furnace, the God we serve is able to deliver us from it…but even if he does not, we want you to know, Your Majesty, that we will not serve your gods or worship the image of gold you have set up." They decided and took a stand, and that is what God expects us to do.

The only tragedy in our journey would be if we walked away from God or if we never learned anything from the journey. But we choose to stand fast in our faith. We choose to continue even stronger and more determined than before. And most important of all, we choose to give God all the glory!

## Lessons Learned

Our time of suffering and trials with ALS taught us these life lessons in faith:

- Suffering teaches us that we can *rejoice* always because God is in the fire with you.
- Suffering causes us to draw closer to God's *presence.*
- Suffering gives us more *strength* (1 Peter 5:10).
- Suffering tests us and causes an even deeper *love* for Christ (Jeremiah 9:7).
- Suffering is God's *refining fire* to give us greater victory (Isaiah 48:10).
- Suffering teaches us about our Savior's *forgiveness* and *grace.*
- Suffering gives us a greater appreciation for the *cross.*
- Suffering tests the *genuineness* of our *faith* (1 Peter 1:7).
- Suffering tests our *hearts* (Proverbs 17:3).
- Suffering is our *offering* of *righteousness* to God (Malachi 3:3).
- Suffering tests the work we have done for Christ (1 Corinthians 3:13).
- Suffering helps us to *comfort others* (2 Corinthians 1:3).
- Suffering teaches us of *God's deliverance* (Job 36:15)
- Suffering teaches us of *Christ's love* for us (1 Peter 2:21).
- Suffering is an *honor* (Acts 5:41).
- Suffering is *shared* with Christ (Romans 8:17).

This list could go on and on because the life lessons we learn from suffering can be added to each and every day. We understand more about suffering with each life lesson and trial we experience. We choose to either learn and grow stronger with each lesson in suffering or we can get bitter and turn away from God. It is my prayer that we all will decide to learn and go deeper with God. The important thing to remember is that we *all will suffer* at some time in our lives. We must be aware and ready when it comes. Too many of my Christian friends were once on fire for God, or seemed to be, and as soon as suffering came into their lives, they blamed God instead of choosing to draw nearer to him. Even though I understand how difficult it can be, it still grieves my spirit to think of so many of them that this has happened to. The three Hebrew children in the book of Daniel had made their choice long before they were faced with the furnace. They determined that they wanted to always walk with God. Take a stand today for Christ, draw a line in the sand and decide that no matter what comes, you are going on with Christ! Make that your heart and soul's declaration today!

# CHAPTER 5

## *The Suffering of the Righteous*

Dear friends, do not be surprised at the painful trial you are suffering as though something strange were happening to you. But rejoice that you participate in the suffering of Christ so you may be overjoyed when his glory is revealed. However, if you suffer as a Christian, do not be ashamed but praise God that you bear that name.
—1 Peter 4:12–13; 16 NIV

## The "Whys" of Suffering

God has been speaking to my heart for the past couple of years on the subject of "suffering." Our family has endured a seven-year battle with a terminal illness, and we have had to face suffering head on with our questions about the "whys" of suffering. What we have found in the asking has not always been the answers we would have desired. What we did find out is that our heavenly Father has faithfully been with us every step, he has surrounded us with his presence that comforts and gives us courage to face every battle. Courage, sometimes, is just to get out of bed and face another horrific day of watching someone you love suffer and waste away in front of your eyes. On this journey, we have found many answers to our questions but just as many questions remain. Our human nature demands answers, but in our spirit, we know that God's ways are not ours, and there are some questions that will remain unanswered until Jesus comes. What we have found to be true is that God is always right there with us, to comfort us and give peace in the trials. In our times of suffering, we have learned to lean on and to trust more completely in the one who has plans to prosper us and give us hope and a future.

> "'For I know the plans I have for you,'
> declares the Lord, 'plans to prosper you and
> not to harm you, plans to give you a hope
> and a future.'"(Jeremiah 29:11 NIV)

We have often heard the comment, *I just don't know how you do it!* As I think about that comment, it brings a smile to my face for several reasons. Even though I know it was always asked from a heart of compassion, just once I would like to have responded with, "What choice do you think we have?" There is not a list of options to choose from when you're thrown into the lion's den; you just hold on to the hope that God will keep the lion's mouth shut just a little while longer!

## Shadrach, Meshach, and Abednego (Daniel 3)

My favorite story in the Old Testament is about the three Hebrew children. You know the story, the one where King Nebuchadnezzar had a ninety-foot tall golden statue made of himself. The people were summoned when the statue was completed for a dedication ceremony. At the celebration, a decree was read that said, "When you hear the music of the harp and the lyre, you are to bow down and worship the idle of the king or be thrown into the fiery furnace." The three Hebrew children had long ago made their choice to stand firm in their faith no matter what the outcome. You can be assured that they had made their decisions and drawn a line in the sand long before this moment of confrontation arrived. They told the king that they would only bow down and worship their God and no one else. They declared that their God was able to save them even if the king were to throw them into the fiery furnace, *but even if God did not save them*, they were going to stay true to him. It angered the king, so he had them make the fire seven times hotter than usual. It was so hot that the guards that threw the three boys in the furnace perished from the heat.

We should all have such confident faith! And when they came out of the fire that day, God showed up and showed himself strong because the boys did not even smell like smoke! But my favorite part of that story is that when the king investigated the furnace, there were four people walking around. God was in there with them! And that is what our family has discovered, no matter how heated the battle becomes, God is always in it with you! He may not choose to take you out of your circumstance, *you might have to go through the fire to get to your victory*, but he has promised to always be right there with you.

God will always get the glory when we remain faithful. In our account of the three children, Shadrach, Meshach and Abednego, King Nebuchadnezzar was amazed when he called for the boys to come out of the furnace and there was not a hair on their head that had been harmed. To the king's surprise, the young men did not even smell like smoke! Then the king said,

"Praise be to the God of Shadrach, Meshach, and Abednego who has sent his angel and rescued his servants! They trusted in him and defied the king's command and were willing to give up their lives rather than serve or worship any god except their own God. Therefore, I decree that the people of any nation or language who say anything against the God of Shadrach, Meshach, and Abednego be cut into pieces and their houses to turned into piles of rubble for no other god can save in this way." (Daniel 3:29)

Then the king promoted the three young men. God gave them victory that day even though they still had to be thrown into the furnace. There is a great lesson in that for all of us.

## Good News in Suffering

> "How lovely on the mountain are the
> feet of those who bring good news,
> announcing peace, proclaiming news of
> happiness, our god reigns." (Isaiah 52:7)

Even in our suffering, there is good news. Good news that God still reigns and is in charge no matter what the outcome. Good news that God never leaves us or forsakes us. Good news that our obedience plays a part in God's will. Because the three were obedient, the king believed in their God. The rules of an entire kingdom were changed. There is good news in knowing that in our obedience, God is glorified! There is good news knowing that in suffering, sin's price was paid for us all. We have good news because the Word of God says that when we suffer, we sin no more. Good news because we know and understand the need for suffering. Good news because we are prepared for suffering, and suffering will not catch us unaware. Good news because we know Jesus suffered and paid the price for our sin. Good news that we can understand the mystery of suffering. And good news because we know God will walk through the fire with us!

I have read the last chapter and know I am victorious! That is the best news ever!

> "Therefore, since Christ suffered in his body,
> arm yourselves also with the same attitude
> because he who has suffered in his body is done
> with sin. As a result, he does not live the rest
> of his earthly life for evil human desires but
> rather for the will of God." (1 Peter 4:1–2)

The word of God tells us that when we suffer for the sake of the cross, we are done with sin. It is in the suffering that we will be able to resist the schemes of the devil. As we daily take up the cross of Christ, sin's hold on us will diminish. When we are obedient, even to suffering, we will, by God's amazing grace, be able to stand strong like the three Hebrew children. Whenever we resist the temptations of the flesh, our old nature, it causes suffering. For example, with someone who is an addict, it will take suffering to overcome the addiction and sin nature. In our day-to-day life as Christians, we must deny the flesh to the point of suffering. No pain, no gain so to speak! We make choices all the time to deny the flesh. When we resist saying something, we know we should not. When we make good choices, that will cause others to make fun of us. When we choose to eat right. There are many ways each day we are given the choice of obedience. Some choices will cause us to suffer in the flesh, some in our spirit, and some in our relationships. But anytime we make the decision to follow the narrow way of obedience, it will strengthen our faith and walk with Christ.

## No Turning Back

We all have come to the decision, somewhere in the timeline of our faith that there is no turning back. Some of us know exactly when we made that decision, and others just know that is what they believe. For me, I remember the exact moment I made that choice for my life. It was back in the '80s in the living room of the church parsonage where we were living at the time. We had gone through a difficult time and almost lost one of our children. I knew the circumstances had been caused by Satan, trying to discourage and make our family turn away from God's will. I made my choice that day to draw my line in the sand. Right then and there, I told Satan, with my fist shaking in his face, no matter what he threw at me, I would not turn my back on my Lord and Savior. I would continue to trust in him with everything in me! I know that loving and serving God is the deepest desire of my heart and life. Let me just warn you, even though *Satan is a defeated foe, he will never give up.* My family and I have kept our resolve through many trials since that day. In my heart, the choice has been made and there is no turning back!

Also, in answer to the question of "I just don't know how you do it?" Our family discovered one of the mysteries of suffering. That when we are faced with suffering, God blesses us with an extra measure of his Holy Spirit's power to give us the strength and endurance needed for the battle. In 1 Peter 4:14, it tells us that when we suffer, the Spirit of God's glory is revealed and rests on us in a special way. We found that God's glory filled our home with his presence and power like we had never known. In your time of suffering, you get a little taste of what heaven will be like. God's love is not dependent on our circumstance, his love is unconditional and constant through the good times and the bad. He has promised to never leave us, and our family can testify to that! We are told in scripture to not be surprised when suffering comes. That means, be ready because it is going to happen.

I have talked to others going through terminal illness and suffering, and what we discovered when comparing notes was that in some ways, it is harder for those not in the battle because they have not been given the extra measure of the Spirit and glory of God. God only gives the extra help when needed. That extra help from his Spirit is the answer to how we got through the suffering.

God tells us to be prepared and even *expect* suffering. Then when suffering comes, we will not be caught off guard. We will be ready to face the battle head on. I wish I could tell you that is how I handled the suffering, but it was not. I was like so many Christians that get caught off guard and swept into the flurry of asking God why even demanding he give us an answer.

God's word takes it a step farther and tells us to *rejoice* in our suffering. I have always been troubled with Paul when he tells us to rejoice in suffering. But I have to say, God has also revealed that mystery to our family. We *can* rejoice because God is always with us. We can rejoice in knowing that we must be doing something right for our enemy to attack us in such a way. We can rejoice because in our suffering, God will show us unexplainable mysteries and reveal a deeper meaning of his word to us. We can rejoice because God promises us in his word that suffering causes us to grow spiritually and in character. We can rejoice because we know that God is at work and will cause all things, even the bad, to work for good in us. Even now, as I look back, I am amazed at all that God did for his glory and our good during Gary's illness. I stand in awe at the strength God gave me, both physically and spiritually, to do what needed to be done to care for Gary. We serve an incredible God that is always at work in our lives to help us, give us strength and courage, and stand with us during our toughest moments in life. We can rejoice because we are not caught off guard but can take up the cross of Christ and his suffering for the glory of God!

It is amazing to me how the theme of suffering is all through every book of the Bible, yet we can miss it so easily when we are not taught or we do not read the Word or we are blinded by the enemy. So often, we read the Word just looking for the promises and blessings, and that is all right. But the Word is balanced, and with every promise, there is something we must do. With every blessing, there is an "if you will do this" you will be blessed! Always read God's word with an open mind and teachable spirit that searches for the truth of his riches.

## You Must Know Your Enemy to be Victorious

Church, it is vital to our survival that we realize we have a very real enemy. God's word tells us that Satan is like a roaring lion, prowling around trying to kill, steal, and destroy us. Our lives are on the battle line every day. There are forces of good and evil warring over your soul. And to be victorious, we must be aware of both our God and Savior as well as the enemy of our soul.

> "Your enemy, the devil, prowls around
> like a roaring lion looking for someone to
> devour. Resist him, standing firm in your
> faith because you know that your brothers
> throughout the world are going through the
> same kind of suffering." (1 Peter 5: 8–9 NIV)

*Satan will never give up* even though he knows he is defeated. Satan sees that we do not always realize he is a defeated foe, and he uses our lack of knowledge or obedience against us. God has given us all power and authority, but most of us do not walk or live in the rights God has given us. We fall so short of walking in victory as more than conquerors. Satan's battle plan is to take as many people to hell with him as he can. God on the other hand wants to give us abundant life and eternity.

> "The thief (Satan) comes only in order to steal
> and kill and destroy. I have come that they may
> have and enjoy life and have it in abundance (to
> the full till it overflows)."(John 10:10 AMP)

The body of Christ needs to understand and embrace suffering and be ready for it when it comes because it will come to us all. The church will be persecuted more and more in the last days, and God wants us ready. In this passage, as well as the entire book of 1 Peter, Peter is not only telling us that the followers of Christ will *suffer* but that we should *count it an honor and rejoice in the suffering*. You might think that this is impossible to attain such a faith to be able to rejoice in suffering. But we must remember that God's word is true, and we, as Christians, have built our lives on our faith in the truth of the Word. Somewhere, we are missing a key that will unlock the mystery and show us the complete truth of this passage.

Believers have gotten the idea that we should never have to suffer. We think that we can just pray and ask for anything, so we ask to be spared of all the suffering. I mean, after all, the Word tells us we have not because we ask not so all we need to do is ask, right? How many times have I prayed to God to keep my children and grandchildren out of a situation and then proceed to tell God exactly what needs to be done to fix it? So many I cannot keep track! How arrogant are we to think we know more than God in telling him just exactly how to fix everything and everyone! We are supposed to ask God for our needs, but what we ask must to be in line with God's Word and the purpose of his heart. I might want a million dollars, which God has been known to give, but God is only going to answer a prayer like that if, number one, it is what he thinks is best for us and two, if it will glorify our heavenly Father.

We always need to remember that God is sovereign, and the final word is up to him. We need to trust him enough to accept his answer as well as his timing. God has a perfect plan for our lives, and we must trust that he knows what is best. Remember the Israelites and their journey to the promise land. It was a twelve-day journey that took forty years of wandering for God to teach them what they needed to know. We read about the Israelites and think that those people were stubborn and just were not teachable. But look at us, we are much the same when it comes to learning and trusting the things of God. Our human nature wants to be in control and to do things our own way. That is why we have to retrain or renew our minds daily in God's Word to learn to trust, lean, and depend on God and "his plan" for our lives.

## God Got My Attention

God seems to get my attention in the strangest places and at the weirdest times. I was at the salon getting my nails done, it was a new nail technician that I had only gone to a few times. I really liked her and soon discovered that she was a believer. It seemed strange to me to meet another believer in a place filled with Buddha statues and bamboo. As she was doing my nails, she was asking questions about Gary. I had been going to this salon for several years, and they all knew about Gary having ALS. This newfound friend and sister in Christ said to me, "You know, God has chosen you and Gary to suffer." I just looked at her in surprise and bewilderment. You know, that look of a "deer in headlights!" She went on to say that we had been chosen because God knew we were strong enough to get through it and that we would give him the glory. I thanked her and went home that day to ponder what she had said. I was not sure it sounded scriptural because I had never heard suffering taught that way in church. But God had used her to plant that seed in my heart at a time when I needed it most. She left the shop shortly after that, and I never saw her again.

It had been strange at how quickly she had come into my life and how quickly she was gone. I began to search the scriptures, but it was not until many months later I was listening, on YouTube, to Francis Chan speak at my grandson's college, Liberty University. Francis was teaching from 1 Peter 4 on suffering. What he taught that day was exactly what the nail technician had told me months before. I listened to that service, repeatedly, to get that teaching in my spirit. God tells us that he sometimes allows suffering to cause us to grow spiritually and to glorify the Father. Now that I understand; I see that theme all through God's word. How did I ever miss it? It is surprising how we can see something so clear in God's Word when we need it most.

> "So then, those who suffer according to God's
> will should commit themselves to their faithful
> Creator and continue to do good."(Daniel 4:19)

Can it really be God's will for us to suffer? If we read and believe his Word, yes, it can be in his plan. It was God who allowed Job to suffer. You see, we serve a loving heavenly Father that knows the number of our days. He knows our future, and he is always preparing us for when the suffering comes. You can be sure that he is always working with our best interests in mind. He promises us a hope and future. It just may not be how you saw your future. So, sometimes, we need to recalibrate our faith to line up with the Word and our life. Often our idea of what God wants for us is not in line with what we want. Gary and I thought we had our future all planned out. But God had another assignment for us that stretched our faith and grew us spiritually while glorifying Father God. There was nothing wrong with our plan, but God's plan is better and always perfect. "His plan" touched lives and gave more glory to the Father than our original plan. His plan is always about salvation and bringing glory to his kingdom.

# Can We Be Thankful in Our Suffering?

Christians in America have developed a "theology of entitlement." The reason I say America is because if you have ever been in a third world country, you realize that our fellow brothers and sisters in Christ in many parts of our world pray and are thankful for their daily "needs" to be met. They rejoice in one meal a day and a roof over their heads. When Gary and I were in Haiti on one of our mission trips there, I could not get over how thankful the children were to get the same noon meal everyday of rice and beans. When they went through the line to get their food, they held on tight with both hands to that precious plate of food. There was no playing around, they were so serious that it caught my attention. For most of them, this would be their only meal for the day. When we passed out pencils and balloons at their school, you would have thought we had given them gold! They had to often share one pencil with the entire class. They cherished and were thankful for every blessing they got!

Look around in the USA, we have storage units on every corner filled with all the "stuff" we cannot fit into our homes, and we still think we need more! I must confess to feeling entitled. Whenever bad things happen to my family, the first thing I would do was list all we had done for God and question why this is happening to us. Sound familiar? I would guess I am not alone in this kind of thinking.

Let us look at suffering from another angle. We all know and agree that God allows the righteous to suffer because he tells us that in the Word. We have seen and experienced suffering in our own lives. All you need do is open your Bible. You will find the righteous suffering from Genesis to Revelations. We know God is a good heavenly Father that wants the best for us and gives us perfect gifts. Are we like the Haitian children *thankful* for what God gives us or do we act like spoiled children when God does not answer our prayers with, when, and what we want? When was the last time you thanked God for your everyday blessings? The things we take for granted, like our meals, clothes, homes, cars, the ability to walk, talk, breathe, and run! We get so caught up in our busyness that we forget to be thankful for the basic things in our life that we take for granted. Because

Gary lost all his bodily functions, we quickly learned to be thankful for the ones he still had and grieved with each loss. But it taught us to be thankful for the little things, like being able to eat, drink, walk, talk, sing, praise, digest food, use our hands. I could go on and on because these were all things Gary lost in the process of his disease. But I am thankful that we learned not to take our body for granted. We are truly fearfully and wonderfully made by the hand of God!

## Suffer and Continue to Do Good

Back to our question, why does he allow suffering? I would go a step further and suggest that God sometimes orchestrates the suffering. Just read the book of Job. Job is not often read or preached from because our views on "suffering sermons" rank right up there with sermons on tithing and holiness. But God has not kept suffering as a secret, in fact, he spells it out for us in Romans.

> "We also rejoice in our sufferings because we know that suffering produces perseverance, perseverance character, and character hope. And hope does not disappoint us because God has poured out his love into our hearts by the Holy Spirit, whom he has given us." (Romans 5:3–5)

> "So then, those who suffer according to God's will should commit themselves to their faithful Creator and continue to do good." (1 Peter 4:19)

The Apostle Paul has not always been one of my favorite people. He often says things that challenge my faith. But as I journey through this life and experience more of life and hopefully have gained some spiritual maturity, I have so much more respect for my brother Paul. He certainly did not come into his spiritual maturity easy in life. He is our perfect example of life lived as a "sacrifice of praise." He learned to rejoice and praise God while in jail and shackled by chains. What a great image that is for us to learn from. We often allow the shackles or cares of life keep us bound in a prison of our own making. When we experience problems in life, we are often too focused on the problem and that takes our focus off Christ. We find it easier to talk about our problems than to pray. The more we talk about the problem, we give Satan a stronger hold on us. Prayer will accomplish more than complaining every time!

In these verses, we can see why God allows suffering. It is to build up our endurance, our character, and hope. All good reasons, but I still hear you asking "why." God knows our future, and he knows what we are going to need to be ready for what is coming, he is preparing us for battle daily. Just like our military prepares every day to be ready to defend our country. God is preparing his army. We must never forget that we are in a war daily over our souls. God wants us to live an abundant life and be victorious while Satan's objective is to destroy us. Never forget you have an adversary that is roaming around trying to use your every weakness against you. God allows trials to make us stronger. Here is another way to look at it. At times, parents let their children make mistakes so they will learn from their mistake. We cannot be with our children 24-7, and so as they get older, we start to back away and allow them to make their own choices and learn from them even when they make a mistake. It is the same way with God. He wants us to grow and mature in our faith so that when the trials of your life happen, and they will happen, you are prepared.

It still amazes me how messed up our theology can get as we live our lives in service to God. But in my life, I have had many hard knocks that have caused me to search the Word of God for the truth and the answer. It is sad to think that so many people who attend church every Sunday never open their Bibles to discover the love letter God has written to them and the richest treasures of life they will ever know. We rely on our ministers and other people to tell us what to believe without checking it out against the truth of God's Word. They are also missing out on the excitement and joy of how God will speak to us personally through his Word. God reminds us that we are more than conquerors through him in this life. That means right now! And that word *more* means that the battle has already been won! That should excite you!

> "For we are more than conquerors through
> him who loved us." (Romans 8:37 NIV)

We fail in life when we neglect our relationship with Christ. It is only in Christ that we can experience and know the love of God. I am convinced that when we are equipped with God's love, we can conquer anything that life throws at us.

We find out in the Word that *faithfulness* to God does not guarantee believers they will never have trouble in life. In fact, when you ask Christ into your life, look out! That is what stirs the devil up, and he will immediately start his attacks on you. In Acts 28:16, we read where Paul, after being beaten, thrown in prison, in chains, and shipwrecked, finally made it to Rome, his mission. But he was still on house arrest. He had one setback after another. Paul remained a faithful servant, doing his best to be obedient, and yet God did not make his way easy. God often takes us a route we would never seek on our own, but we know all things work for good for those called according to his purpose.

> "And we know that in all things, God works for
> the good of those who love him, who have been
> called according to his purpose." (Romans 8:28)

## Godly People Suffer and Find Victory

The Bible gives many examples of godly people who experienced suffering and were still victorious. Joseph, David, Job (the poster boy for suffering), Jeremiah, and Paul just to mention a few. Our greatest example of suffering and victory is Christ's death on the cruel cross of Calvary. He suffered everything we will ever have to suffer. He took our shame and sin and suffered when he was innocent, all for us. He suffered and became our victorious champion!

"To this you were called because Christ suffered
for you, leaving you an example, that you
should follow in his steps." (1 Peter 2:21 NIV)

Another reason we suffer is because of the fall of man. The fall caused sin, suffering, and death to enter the world. Because of Adam and Eve's sin, all humans are born into the world with a sinful nature. It is because of that old nature that Jesus died as a perfect sacrifice for our sins. He paid the price for our sin debt. A price no one else could pay.

We also suffer at times from the consequences of our own sin. The word says we reap what we sow, that is a biblical principal we all live with. If we have unhealthy habits, we might suffer illness; if we drive reckless, we might have an accident; if we do not manage our finances well, we will experience money problems. We must always seek godly wisdom and stay in agreement with God's Word. We also suffer because we live in a corrupt world where we see the effects of sin all around us. And finally, we suffer at the hands of Satan because he is the god of this world till Jesus returns. We need to remember that Satan's rule is only temporary. He continues only by God's permission until Jesus returns.

"The god of this world has blinded the minds
of the unbelieving so that they might not see
the light of the gospel of the glory of Christ,
who is the image of God." (2 Corinthians 4:4)

## Job's Suffering—Good Tests

We see the suffering of Job, who was a God-fearing man, as a test. When we hear the word *suffering*, we immediately think of it as a negative thing to avoid at all cost. None of us want to suffer. But as you understand God's heart and purpose for allowing suffering, you can begin to see how we can rejoice and see victory in the suffering. As the body and bride of Christ, God wants us to be ready and prepared for his return. We can look on as other people go through suffering and think that will never happen to me, but let me assure you, we all will suffer at some point in our lives. No one is immune or gets a get-out-of-suffering card from God.

God allows what I call "good tests" at times so *we will know the strength of our faith*! When my husband was the senior pastor at a church in the Washington, DC, area, our church had over fifteen countries represented in our congregation. We loved being a part of the international community. We loved our congregation and respected them. They were all hard workers, many having multiple jobs. They loved and appreciated living in this country where they had religious freedom. However, there were challenges because of the diversity. They all had differing opinions of what the pastor's wife should be and do because of our different cultural upbringing. One of my weaknesses, at the time, was that I was a people pleaser.

One Sunday morning after the church service was over, one of the ladies stopped me in the front of the church, with many people still standing around fellowshipping after the service, and began to tell me, in not a quiet tone, that I was an awful mother because of a situation that had happened to my daughter. This lady proceeded to tell me just what I needed to be doing to correct the problem. But the amazing thing to me was the fact that I stayed and felt so calm with every accusing word! Even while she was pointing her finger in my face, I was thinking to myself, *Why am I so calm?* It was a strange occurrence for me. I am not an outspoken person, but like any mother, you never attack my family, or I will tell you exactly what I think in their defense. The thing about this incident (many pastor's wives will relate), the lady did not have all the facts. She was referring to a very private family tragedy we had suffered but had not made known to the church because of the personal nature of what had happened. She was not aware of the event that had taken place but evidently thought she knew what was going on enough to get involved. I listened until she was finished berating me in front of everyone and calmly and lovingly told her that I was sorry she felt that way. And I walked away, still amazed at how calm I was.

When I told Gary (the calm person in our marriage) about what had happened, he wanted to get in the car and go to her home and confront her, but to do that we would need to explain it all to her, and it was none of her business. That was a "good test" for me. When God allowed that to happen, it showed me my spiritual growth. I rejoiced in knowing that the Holy Spirit in me had handled it well and passed the test that day! That test served to strengthen me, and our time at that church taught me to be a God pleaser and not a people pleaser. The testing brought *victory* in my life. God's purpose in the testing is always to bring about spiritual maturity in us.

As believers, we also suffer because we have the mind of Christ. Having the mind of Christ, we see things the way God sees them, and we value and love the things God loves. We also hate the things God hates. Having the mind of Christ means that we know and understand his will and purpose. We see things the way God does. It also means understanding his holiness as well as how awful sin is and what it can do to a person.

> "For who has known the mind of the Lord
> that he may instruct him?But we have the
> mind of Christ." (2 Corinthians 2:16)

Because we have the mind of Christ, our views are usually radically different from the world. To have the mind of Christ and be one with him, we also share in his sufferings. Christ is our greatest example of suffering. He suffered everything we have or will ever suffer. He was blameless and took on our sins. He died for *my* sins, for *my* shame, for *my* rebellion, for *my* old nature to be made new. So, how could I ever think, that with Christ as my example all through life, I would not have to suffer like he suffered? We often forget to count the cost of living for Christ. Salvation is a gift and one we can never earn. Jesus had to pay that price for us. He was the spotless lamb. Living for Christ is another matter; we will need to count the cost as we take up the cross of Christ. Suffering is part of that cost, but God's economics are always in our favor. As we keep our eyes on Jesus, our reward is eternal life in heaven in the presence of God our heavenly Father.

Suffering is an honorable and good thing because if we are worthy enough to be called Christians, we must be ready to lay down our life and pick up that cross of suffering, knowing that it will make us stronger and ultimately Christ will be glorified. When we learn to embrace suffering for God's glory, we will be an unstoppable force for God's kingdom.

> "The apostles left the Sanhedrin rejoicing
> because they had been counted worthy of
> suffering disgrace for the name." (Romans 5:3)

As we have read in Romans 5:3, Paul lists suffering as one of the blessings of our salvation in Christ. Are you seeing the victory yet? It takes some time to digest it because it is not our usual way of thinking, "Oh great, let us go suffer! Yeah!" But God is telling us that it should be just like my friend at the nail salon had shared with me, that God calls us to suffer for our own good and his glory.

## Another "God Moment" at the Nail Salon

Our other spa adventure was when I took Gary with me for the first time. I had talked him into getting a pedicure. Which I will tell you took some talking! The ladies at the salon were excited to meet him because I had told them so much about our ALS journey. They all hovered around him and helped him from his wheelchair to the spa chair. He was getting the "royal treatment." When he was done getting his pedicure, I saw the lady who was a Christian, the one that had witnessed to me, go over to him and ask him to pray for her. Of course, I quickly jumped in and told her that he could not speak, like she did not already know that fact! She calmly told me she understood, but he could lay hands on her and pray. Wow, did I feel bad for interrupting. God has a way of saying just sit back and see what I can do.

Gary proceeded to pray for her, and then, right there in the middle of the spa, a prayer line started to form. Business stopped as the other technicians gathered around Gary's wheelchair, and before

I knew what was happening, he was praying for them all! This is a man who can no longer speak, but these ladies had the faith and trust to ask him to lay hands on them and pray for their needs. We were experiencing the *joy in the journey* of our suffering right there in the spa! Gary's suffering touched the lives and hearts of so many. His ALS journey took us outside the church walls, and we were able to minister to people we would never have been able to any other way. God is so incredibly good. It is such an adventure to trust and walk with him.

## The Word of God and the Full Gospel

Christians in the end times are going to depend on ministers who do not preach the full gospel message out of fear of losing people in their congregations. God warns us in his word that in the last days, pastors will only preach what we want to hear or what tickles our ears and makes us feel good.

> "For the time will come when they will not
> endure sound doctrine butafter their own
> lusts shall they heap to themselves teachers,
> having itching ears. And they shall turn
> away their ears from the truth and shall
> be turned into fables." (2 Timothy 4)

The reason so many pastors preach a partial gospel is because they want to be politically correct and not offend anyone for fear they will then leave the church. Which is an understandable fear if you look at the current statistics that tell us there are six to ten thousand churches that close each year in America. And over seventeen hundred pastors each month leave the ministry. Preaching the full gospel of Jesus Christ is not for the faint hearted. In fact, you must have a determination in ministry, much like our friends, the three Hebrew children had in their faith, that no matter what the outcome, we will go all the way with Christ! So, most pastors stay on more neutral, easy-to-swallow subjects and steer away from controversial subjects like tithing, abortion, suffering, the end times, God's wrath, judgment day, prophecy, holiness, and so many more. We need to understand just how important the Word of God is in our life. God's Word is the plumb line in our life because it is how we measure righteousness and our relationship with God.

Many pastors fear losing congregates if they share the full truth of the gospel. Often, we hear that when we give our life to Christ, everything will be great and you will have perfect peace and joy. It is easy to teach the love, peace, and joy of Jesus, and that is true. But it is not the whole truth. The whole truth is that when we give our heart to God, it stirs up the enemy, and he wages an all-out assault on our life and family. We need to let new believers know the truth in love and then allow the Holy Spirit to do the convicting. God's Word is not fully understood at the time of our conversion, but God will reveal the truth as the need arises and as we grow spiritually. It remains our calling and responsibility as men and women in the ministry to teach the entirety of God's Word and not pick and choose only what is palatable. God wants us to embrace suffering.

Most new believers will be totally blown away by that concept; let us face it, the suffering spoke of in the Bible is hard for mature Christians to comprehend. But it is still our responsibility to teach the whole truth and leave it to God to touch hearts as needed. But how dare we leave the believers unaware of the enemy and his tactics? It is the same as tithing. Many pastors steer clear of teaching it because it often causes dissention, but when we do not teach tithing, we are robbing the body of Christ of their God-given blessings of the principle of giving. When suffering is not taught, we rob the body of Christ of being overcomers in this life. When we embrace suffering, we are unstoppable. And because we *all will suffer* at some time in our life, so why not equip the body of Christ with the truth so they will be an unstoppable force for God's kingdom?

## Missionaries Who Suffer—Still Rejoice in God's Presence

When we are suffering, that is when we sense God's presence the most powerful in our life. Over a decade ago, there was a group of Korean missionaries traveling from Kabul to Kandahar that were captured by the Taliban and tortured. They were in captivity for quite a while. The Taliban leader was going to behead one of them, and the senior pastor of the group offered up himself to be killed. But another one of the pastors said, "No, take me, I am the elder here." And yet another pastor in the group said, "No, take me because that pastor has never been ordained." They were all willing and trying to save one another, that is love! The last pastor who spoke was beheaded. Shortly after that time, they were rescued and released. A few years later while being interviewed, one of the pastors said that it may sound strange, but he would gladly go back to that time again because it was where he had felt the presence of God the most powerful in his life. Surprisingly, I understand what he is talking about because our home was so filled with the presence and peace of God during Gary's illness. It was the beautiful presence of God that everyone who visited our home felt also, hard to explain.

In Acts 7:54–60, we read where Stephen, as he was being stoned, said he saw Christ standing (not sitting as normally spoke of) at the right hand of God the Father. Jesus had stood to welcome the first to be martyred for confessing Christ before men.

> "But Stephen, full of the Holy Spirit,
> looked up to heaven and saw the glory of
> God and Jesus standing at the right hand
> of God. 'Look,' he said, 'I see heaven
> open and the Son of Man standing at the
> right hand of God.'" (Acts 7:55–56)

## Gary Seeing and Meeting Jesus in Our Room

Gary and I could both relate to what the missionary had shared. During Gary's illness, we sensed the presence of God in our lives and home like no other time before or since. God will always show himself strongest when most needed.

One evening a few days before Gary died, our family was gathered in our bedroom like we always did. We were laughing and talking while Gary slept; I was holding his hand like I had so often. He was never awake now due to the medication the hospice nurse had prescribed for him. All the machines were shut off, at his request, he was ready to go home. Suddenly, his eyes were wide open, and he was gazing up at the ceiling in our room. I am not sure why, except for the expression on his face. I asked him, "Gary, do you see Jesus?"

He turned his head slightly toward me, his eyes still wide open in recognition, smiled, and nodded yes and immediately went back to sleep. There was no doubt in my mind that in his darkest hour, he had seen Jesus. I will treasure that moment forever, and I thank God for sharing it with our family while we were all present in the room. It gives such comfort knowing that he saw Jesus. There was a holy peace in the room that night. We had been praying that his passing would be easy because he had suffered so much for seven years with ALS. He went from a healthy 180 pounds down to 70 pounds. He was just skin and bones. My strong, healthy warrior and defender was left with a body racked in pain. We wanted him to be out of pain and suffering and be home with his Jesus. Even that brought suffering to us in his loss. But I can truthfully tell you, like those Korean missionaries, during Gary's illness, we both felt the closest to God we had ever felt.

That is my answer to all of you who asked us how we did it every day. You see, when you are in the middle of the fire, God is always there right beside you. He gives you supernatural strength and faith like you never thought you could have. Even now, as I look back, I am amazed at all we went through and all the medical things we had to learn and do, like cleaning his trach, and for Gary, every day was a new challenge. But God was always with us, forever show-ing himself strong on our behalf.

I would not want anyone to go through what Gary and our family had to endure, but I can tell you that we are stronger, braver, more courageous, and more on fire for Jesus than ever before. I have learned to see things more in the light of eternity than just the here and now. I guess you might say God has given me a new *eternal per-spective*. I am convinced that Jesus will be coming soon, and that is why he wants us to understand his message on suffering, it is vital to the body of Christ so we can live *victoriously* as overcomers in this life!

## Stand Firm on God's Word

God's Word has so many layers to discover in our life, we will never fully understand all the mysteries found in the Word. But I am convinced that when we need to have a deeper understanding, God opens a little more for us and reveals exactly what we need to know. God's word is from everlasting to everlasting and never changes. We can read something in the Word that we have read hundreds of times and find new depth to the meaning that we did not see before. What we know and understand changes with our life experiences and our spiritual maturity. Let me explain what I mean using my favorite Old Testament story of Shadrach, Meshach, and Abednego, the three Hebrew children who were thrown into the fiery furnace because they refused to bow in worship to a gold statue of King Nebuchadnezzar.

Early in my Christian walk, I loved the resolve of the three for taking a stand and not backing down even in the face of death. They told the king that they would continue to worship their God and that they knew their *God could save them, but even if he did not*, they would still not serve the king or his gods. This made the king mad, and he ordered the furnace to be made seven times hotter than usual. As I matured, both from life experience and in the faith, more in the Lord, I loved the fact that God always goes the extra mile in answering our prayers. He usually gives us more than we ask for or even knew to ask for. In this story, not only did the three live but they came out of the furnace not even smelling like smoke. The three brought glory to God in their suffering and were promoted by the king. At this point in my life, as I read this story, I am excited and blessed by the fact that even though the three were still thrown in the furnace, God was right there in the fire with them. God promises to never leave us, and we can take courage knowing that he is with us during our most difficult trials in life. God's word never changes, but how we read and interpret it does because of our life experiences, spiritual growth, and our need.

Because we all will be tested in our daily walk with Christ, we need to make the choice that we will stand firm in our faith and be confident in Christ. You can be sure that the three Hebrew boys had made their choice long before they stood in front of the king. They never once questioned why this was happening to them, they just knew that God would be with them no matter what if they remained faithful. The word says, having done all just stand, once you have done all you know to do, it is time to just stand firm in your convictions and trust God.

> Therefore, my dear brothers, stand firm. Let
> nothing move you. Always give yourselves
> fully to the work of the Lord because
> you know that your labor in the Lord is
> not in vain." (1 Corinthians 15:58)

We can see the "joy in the journey" of our suffering when we know and understand how much God loves us and wants the best for us. Even when we do not understand the big picture, we can be sure that God does, and he is preparing us for whatever our future holds. Our victory is in Christ alone! Christ in our lives is our only boast. We can never do enough to earn or be worthy of all he has done for us. Just know that he loves you with an everlasting, unconditional, lavish, love!

God might not change your circumstance, but he will see you through to the victory. The victory might not be what you asked for, but it will be God's best for your life. And when God brings about the victory, it will always glorify the Father and his kingdom.

Choose to embrace and rejoice in suffering when it comes, and remember it is for your spiritual growth and God's glory. It would be a shame if we endured the suffering and did not grow or learn from the journey. While hanging on the cross for our sins, Christ could see down through time, and for the *joy* set before him, he endured the cross. He could see the victory his death would purchase for all of creation, and he could rejoice!

I would like to finish the thoughts on suffering by including an article that my oldest daughter, Deanna, wrote on this same topic.

## "I Choose Suffering" by Deanna Tingwald-Higgins

"Lift up your eyes to the heavens, look at the earth beneath; the heavens will vanish like smoke, the earth will wear out like a garment, and its inhabitants die like flies. But my salvation will last forever, my righteousness will never fail" (Isaiah 51:6).

Have you ever felt like a sinking ship being tossed to-and-fro in a relentlessly angry sea? I have. I feel quite certain that I am not alone, I am sure there are others sinking in the raging waters even now. Sometimes, we face the ugly reality of suffering because we have made a bad or possibly several bad decisions, facing consequences that we must resign ourselves to. What happens when the harsh pangs of suffering find us because of circumstances outside of our control, like a ship sailing into unavoidable winds? For the past several years (seven to be exact), our family has been flailing in the open waters of a raging sea, clinging with every bit of strength we can muster to a water-logged life preserver. You see, my dad was diagnosed with a monster of a disease called ALS (amyotrophic lateral sclerosis). This was a death sentence that slowly robbed him of his ability to speak, eat, move, and sometimes even breathe on his own. My mom spent her days tirelessly but lovingly caring for him until the very end. The past couple of years of his life were absolutely excruciating for him. He had constant issues with bed sores and excessive weight loss, pain meds were unable to keep up with his dreadful discomfort. He was trapped inside his own torture chamber day after day after agonizing day. Even during the myriad of feeding and ventilator tubes in his makeshift hospital room in their home, there was a strange peace that accompanied his mighty tempest of suffering.

The peace was one that could only be gifted from one source, Jesus. My dad was a pastor before being forced to retire due to his inability to speak not long after his diagnosis. This was a man who had always walked out his faith; he was an unassuming shepherd that loved God and people passionately. His ability to minister to others was done with a uniquely quiet strength that I have never seen in another individual. So, that is how he faced his deadly last few years, choosing suffering with a quiet and peaceful strength that only comes from God. I have learned so much watching his love for Jesus and others around him, even while he was on his bed of affliction, a prisoner in his own body. Those who came to visit him would find themselves encouraged and strengthened in their faith.

Life is so strange sometimes. I wish my dad wouldn't have had to spend the last few years of his life the way he did. I wanted him to be able to throw the football with my boys, to wrestle on the floor and chase them around the house until they were out of breath from laughter. But that was not the life we were given. To say I spent many hours questioning and wrestling with God would be a gross under-statement. Somehow through the pain and suffering, we had count-less holy encounters with our Creator, times that only he was able to issue the strength, courage, and ability we needed to keep moving on his terrifying journey. My faith was reinforced and even invigorated in the saddest and constant sorrow of loss. It was an unexpected and divine gift that came out of an atrocious season of suffering.

My heavenly Father faced suffering I cannot even imagine. My earthly father faced suffering that I could barely find the courage to watch toward the end. Not only did Jesus endure horrible suffering for us but he chose it. He chose it so that you and I could be free from sin. I do not understand it, but I am so humbled and grateful for it.

I choose suffering because it was and is God's plan. I choose suffering because he met me at that place of exhaustion and made me a better follower of him. He used my dad as a beautiful vessel to teach me and countless other the lesson of loving Christ deeper even when suffering.

I live by the ocean. It is beautiful and frightening at the same time. This life is beautiful, but suffering will come, embrace it, learn from it. Be stronger because of it. Allow Christ to meet you in your most dreadful storm that life will certainly throw at you. My dad did, and he taught me to embrace it through the power of our heavenly Father, the prince of peace.

> "This life is beautiful, but suffering will come, embrace suffering, learn from it, be stronger because of it."
>
> —Deanna Tingwald-Higgins

> "Suffering is the textbook that teaches who we really are. Suffering is God's choicest tool to molding our character."
>
> —Joni Eareckson

> "When we learn to embrace suffering for God's glory, we will be an unstoppable force for God's kingdom."
>
> —Vickie Tingwald

# CHAPTER 6

## *The Hard Things In Life*

> Sovereign Lord, you have made the heavens and the earth by your great power and outstretched arm. Nothing is too hard for you.
>
> —Jeremiah 32:17

## The Hard Things

GOD WILL ALWAYS ask us to do the hard things in life. Remember what he asked Noah to do, build an ark. That was no small task to build an ark big enough to last an unknown amount of time. An ark so gigantic it would be able to hold two of every animal on earth. And that is not even including all the supplies needed for that unknown amount of time. Supplies enough for the humans as well as all those animals. Noah's friends called him crazy and mocked him because there had never been rain like Noah was predicting. Most of us would just have went the other direction if given a monumental assignment like this from God. We would probably tell God to find somebody else. Noah must have felt like that too, but he wanted to be obedient to God.

I can hear my excuses now, "God, I know nothing about building an ark, there must be others more qualified. God, it will be impossible to gather all the animals and build an ark so large. God, my family will never get on board with this, they will call me crazy. And, God, what will my neighbors think?" I am sure I would come up with many more excuses, until I would talk myself right out of obeying God. I mean, isn't that what we do when God asks us to do the hard things that seem impossible? What about when he asked Moses to lead the Israelites out of captivity in Egypt? Moses had excuses why he could not do it, but eventually, his desire to be obedient won.

In the Matthew chapter 19, you will remember the rich young ruler who came to Jesus and asked, "Teacher, what good thing must I do to get eternal life?"

Jesus replied, "There is only one who is good. If you want to have eternal life, obey the commandments."

The young ruler asked, "Which ones?"

Jesus gave him the list of commands, and the young ruler replied that he had kept them all. Jesus replied, "If you want to be perfect, go, sell your possessions and give to the poor, and you will have treasures in heaven. Then come, follow me."

Jesus had asked the young ruler to do a hard thing, but the young man walked away, without obeying, because he had great wealth. We assume he did not want to hear the answer Jesus gave. Jesus knows our hearts, and he knows what it will take to keep us on the right path, but we must have willing hearts to obey. Jesus knew in the young ruler's heart that his possessions meant more to him than storing treasures in heaven, even his eternal life.

## God Shows Himself Strong

God wants us to be bold and courageous and step out in faith when he asks us to do the hard things in life. God will always ask us to do the difficult things because it is in doing them that we learn to walk by faith and trust him more. If he only gave us easy things that we can accomplish on our own, we would not learn what it is to depend on God and trust him enough to step out of the boat, our comfort zone. Think about the hard things in your life that God has asked you to do and remember how it was empowering to know how much your reliance on God had gotten you through to your victory.

When Gary first shared with me that he felt God was leading him in another direction in ministry, toward the chaplaincy, I panicked. I never minded moving or change, but I just did not see how I fit into the picture. I was a children's pastor, not a prison chaplain. But I knew in my spirit that it was right and it was where God wanted us to go. God was asking me to do a hard thing that would take faith, courage, and trusting him. I still was not thrilled and told God often. But my final prayer of acceptance was, "Okay, God, you know I want to be faithful and I want to support my husband in this new ministry, *but* you will need to show yourself strong on our behalf because my faith is just not where it needs to be for all this. Amen." I have said this so many times, but I need to say it again. From the Amen of that prayer until this very moment, God has shown himself so strong and been there in our lives when we needed him. He has never left us and has truly shown himself strong and faithful in meeting all our needs.

When we started our journey into the chaplaincy, Gary was excited, but I was still apprehensive. To my amazement, God started showing himself strong immediately. We had left the church we had pastored and our home, which was owned by the church, and moved to Chesapeake, Virginia, where the cost of living was better. We needed a home but had no down payment, that did not stop God. We bid on a home, and there were three other bids, all higher than ours. "But God" stepped into the situation, and the sellers chose us because they believed in missions, and we were now US Missionaries in the Assemblies of God. God gave us favor! Then I needed a job since we would have no income while Gary would be raising support. "But God" showed up again, and I not only found a job but one in the children's ministry with health insurance! Then we had a problem with transportation. We only had one vehicle and needed two. Gary needed to travel to churches in our district while I needed to go to my new job. "But God" had the solution we never even thought to pray for, someone gave us a vehicle. By now, I am beginning to trust God more because he has showed up strong every time we had a need.

Later in our chaplaincy journey, we had such a great need that we knew only God could make it happen. We had been working, traveling, sending newsletters, and filling every spare moment doing our best in getting our support raised. After about a year and a half, we got a letter from the US Missions Department in Springfield, letting us know we had to finish raising our support in the next six months. At first, we were caught off guard and knew that we could never make that happen. The US Missions Department sets your support goal. They take into consideration such things as housing, health insurance, car/gas/insurance, travel expense, ministry expense, and general living expenses. That figure is never a small one, it is always based on where you live as well. Living on the east coast is more expensive than the Midwest for example.

Anyway, in our first year and a half, we had only been able to raise about half of our support. The US Missions Department does not want your support raising to linger on too long, which we understood and respected. Gary and I both knew it would be humanly impossible for us to accomplish the goal set before us. We prayed, and surprisingly, it was me who step out in faith this time. I told Gary that God had called him, and now it would be up to God to make this happen. I felt that God had shown himself strong and faithful on our behalf, and he would continue. The ball was in God's court now. We kept on doing what we had been doing and waited and prayed to see what miracle God would perform.

God has never let us down, and this time, he came through big time! Gary had been volunteering at a local jail with a ministry called Southeastern Correctional Ministry. He loved sharing God's word, bringing hope to the inmates. SCM was looking for a new senior chaplain to head up the ministry and approached Gary. Gary turned them down because he did not feel like he had all the qualifications they were looking for, mainly a bachelor's degree. They approached him again, asking him to come in for an interview. Gary was still not sure because it was an interdenominational ministry and not affiliated with our denomination. He was not sure the US Missions Department would allow him to head up such a ministry. I encouraged him to call the missions department and talk to them about the opportunity. We did not even know what the salary for the position would be. The next day, Gary made a call to the Chaplaincy Department, and during the conversation with the head of the Chaplaincy Department, he stopped Gary midsentence and asked him, "Gary, are you asking if you can accept their offer if hired?" Gary answered yes, and he was quickly told that it would be a great opportunity, so, yes, accept it!

Gary went for the interview and was hired on the spot! This was all such a miracle for many reasons. First, the salary offered was exactly the other half of our support needed to get started on the chaplaincy ministry. But to us, the greater miracle, if there is such a thing as a "greater miracle," was that Gary would be stepping into an established ministry in our community. SCM was in over twenty-three facilities in the Hampton Roads area. They ministered to over 8,000 inmates on a weekly basis and had approximately 800 volunteers. We did not have to invent the wheel, it was already rolling! A ministry, like SCM, would have taken us a lifetime to establish, and here it was, God had opened an amazing door for us and all we had to do was take that step of faith and be obedient. It was not a difficult decision; we were just so thankful for God's grace and mercy toward us. He had once again shown himself strong on our behalf! We serve a God of endless patients and compassion!

## Facing the Truth—Doing the Hard Thing

The next thing God would ask of me was one of the most challenging things he had ever asked. I had been praying about what part I was to play in the chaplaincy ministry. I wanted to support Gary as much as time would allow with me working full time. I was able to travel with him occasionally to the churches where he would have services to raise awareness about the need for prison chaplains within our denomination and to raise support. I felt in my spirit that God wanted me to do more, but once again, I would ask, where do I fit into prison ministry? I was asking and waiting to hear from God. I did not have to wait long.

God began to deal with my heart about some deep-seeded issues I was not even aware of that I had never given completely over to him. He reminded me about my brother. My brother, when he was a teenager, made some bad decisions, and he was always in and out of trouble. Finally, one day, he and a friend decided to rob a gas station. They had a gun with them, so when they were arrested, it was for "armed robbery." My brother, because of his bad record, was sentenced to ten years in prison. That sentencing not only affected him, but it affected our entire family. As a young child, I remember we were always visiting him because he was always getting locked up for something. Before I go on, I want to say that my brother eventually got his life straightened out, it took many years and many hardships. He became a good man and helped a lot of others who were dealing with alcohol and other addictions. He died a couple years ago and was saved when he went to meet Jesus. I miss him every day. But when we were kids, it was hard on us to have a brother who was constantly causing chaos in our lives. I had friends in fifth grade who refused to play with me one day at recess because their parents, who I went to church with, found out I had a brother in prison.

When I was a teenager and dating, I had a boyfriend who, all of a sudden, stopped taking me to his house. When I asked why, I was told that his parents had found out about my brother. His father worked at the same factory as my dad and had heard about my brother in the workplace. I learned early on not to talk about or tell anyone about my brother. My grandparents, who were Pentecostal through and through, refused to write my brother while he was in prison because they did not want any of their "church friends" in their small town to find out they had a grandson in prison. When Gary and I started dating, I told him I had a brother who lived in northern Iowa. He did live in northern Iowa, I just left out the part about it being a prison. After we were engaged, my parents told me that I needed to tell Gary the whole truth. I refused because I was sure he would take back the ring and call off our marriage if he knew. I judged him to react just like everyone else in my life had reacted. I was certain I would be rejected once again. The rejections I encountered in my young life had left a scar I had never dealt with.

I eventually told Gary. The moment in time and the place were forever etched in my mind and heart. Like the day the first man walked on the moon, or the Twin Towers fell, or JFK was shot. Anyway, you see what I mean, we all remember where we were and what we were doing. When I told Gary, at first, I giggled a little out of nervousness, and he thought I was kidding. Then I started to cry because I just knew what was coming. He was driving the car, and he just looked at me kind of puzzled and then realized how upset I was. He understood where I was coming from, and the next words out of his mouth, I would learn over the years, were so typically Gary. He said, "Vickie, it's okay, I am not marrying your brother, I am marrying you." And it was settled forever right then and there in that moment never to be discussed as an issue again. I still made him promise not to tell his family out of the same fear of rejection. That is another story, but I can tell you, I never felt an ounce of rejection from his family even after they were told. God reminded me of Gary's response to me in 1968 to ask me to do what he knew would be hard for me in 2003.

## The Whole Truth and Nothing but the Truth

Years had gone by, and I was now a minister's wife, mother, grandmother, and a credentialed minister. The hurts of those early years were safely tucked away for no one to see or disturb. I had carried the baggage of "never feeling like I was good enough" for most of my life. God had slowly and lovingly helped me so much in that area, and I thought it had been healed for good. God has a way of making us deal with things; even when we are not aware, we need a spiritual healing. God reminds us of the difficult things so we will take care of them and give them to him. The hard thing God asked me to do was to share my personal testimony concerning my brother. I had so many excuses of why that would not be possible.

First, I tried to convince myself that request could not possibly be from God. Then I reminded God that I had never shared that part of my personal testimony before. When I was arguing my points before God, I realized what I was saying, and I stopped abruptly and began to ask myself why I had not shared that part of my life as an adult. The answer came immediately, I knew it was out of fear, shame, and not wanting to be rejected. God was asking me to be real and share my story with every church in our district, at least all the ones Gary would have a service at. How could he ask me to put myself out there like that? And am I willing to risk my well-thought-of reputation? I needed to know why I should do that and who would it help anyway

God's answer was just as swift, "Why, because I have asked you." Who? God told me that I did not need to know who and that I would understand later. I had a big decision to make, and if I was going to do this, I wanted to know exactly what I was to share so I would not share more than I needed to. Again, God was quick to respond. He told me that I was to share my entire story and not hold back. Having the desire to be used, I began drafting my testimony.

## The Untold Testimony

We had been in the Potomac District for over fifteen years at this time, so I would be speaking to men and women who had known Gary and I for quite a while. These people I am about to be real with are friends I had never been completely honest with for fear of rejection and feelings of inadequacy. Up to this time in my life, there had not been a need or reason to share that part of my life. But now, God has a purpose and plan that by me sharing my whole story, others will be helped and God will be glorified. I just could not yet see the whole picture and needed to trust God and take that step of faith. One that would change my life forever and touch the hearts of many. God is so loving and knows exactly what we need to be set free from, the insecurities that keep us from our abundant life and victory! I was about to find out just how much I needed this lesson on being real.

When God reminded me about my brother and how Gary reacted when I told him, I finally could see why God had called Gary to the chaplaincy. Because Gary never judged people, he always saw the good in them. He did not judge my brother, in fact, once he met Tommy, they became fast friends. God had chosen Gary to minister to men and women who had made mistakes. Gary never asked them why they were in jail, that was between them and God, he just loved and ministered to them right where they were spiritually. And they loved Chaplain Gary! I was thankful that God had given me a glimpse into his plan. Now I had to trust him in what he was asking me to do.

God also reminded me that it was a prison chaplain that had turned my brother's life around. He got into fights and trouble while in prison. The chaplain finally got his attention and told him that he would have to serve the whole ten years if he did not stop getting into trouble all the time. My brother started attending mass and stopped getting into trouble.

God had settled things in my heart and gave me the reasons why I needed to share my story, but I never would have dreamed the lives that would be touched.

When I stood before the congregation of the first church I spoke at, I was nervous how I would be received. The first congregation was the church we had been ministering at for the last seven years. The points the Lord had shown me to make were these. First, tell them about my brother. Then explain I had never shared about him to anyone because of my fear of rejection. God had also told me to share how that rejection had come from Christians and how a church family should allow each other to be real without fear of rejection. And to my amazement, at each church that I shared my testimony, there was always someone standing in the back wanting to talk to me after the service. They would thank me for having the courage to share and then begin to tell me their story. There were moms, wives, sisters, and friends that would tell me someone in their family or a friend was in jail or had been in jail. The sad realization came to me when they would say that they would never tell their church family or even their pastor for fear of being judged or that their incarcerated family member would be judged when what they needed was prayer. It was the same story at every church. How it must break God's heart when we are judgmental and unforgiving to one another in the family of

God. Of all places we should feel safe and be able to be real, it should be with our brothers and sisters in Christ.

I finally knew and understood why God had asked me to share my story. Not only did it set me free, but it helped countless others to have a voice. Hopefully, our church families had a little better understanding of one another. God can always take the pain in our life and turn it into a blessing when we are willing to allow him to use us. We all have a story to tell, and it is in the telling that we find our freedom, and our story can help others and glorify our heavenly Father.

## My Early Family Life

It has taken other hard things in my life for God to show me what a rich heritage I have in him. When I would hear other people's testimonies, I would always think that I sure do not want to share mine. They might see who I really am. I grew up in a dysfunctional home (we are all a little dysfunctional, I have learned) with a father who was an alcoholic. There were many abuses in our home, but the one that did the most damage was not the physical but the verbal. We were told we could not do anything right. We never received any praise or encouragement. We were made to feel like we were just in the way all the time. I have been able to forgive over the years because I could see that my parents did the best they knew how. My mom was raised by an alcoholic father and a stepmom she felt never wanted her. She left home at fourteen and was unwed and pregnant at fifteen. My dad was raised by legalistic Pentecostal parents that taught him everything was wrong and holiness was what you saw on the outside. My parents did their best to be what they thought were good parents. They were married for fifty-three years. Somehow in all that dysfunction, they taught us to love God even though I never knew them to go to church. I was the fourth of five siblings. All five of us have stayed married for more than fifty years. We all are hard workers and conscientious to a fault. I figure my parents must have done something right.

## Experiencing the Love of God at the Children's Pastors' Conference

Another lesson God taught me was just how much he loved me. When we were ministers on the eastern shore of Maryland in the '90s, I was the children's pastor. Every two years, there was a Children's Pastors' Conference in Springfield, Missouri. One year, I felt I was to attend the conference, but I did not really want to go because I would have to fly there by myself and attend by myself. Gary encouraged me to attend, and I ended up going. I attended the entire weeklong conference and thought it was good, but I still did not see why God was prompting to go. On the last night, there was a BGMC Banquet (Boys and Girls Missionary Crusades). I was excited when I saw that the African Children's Choir was going to be performing. I had seen them twice and loved their energetic music and their testimonies. When the doors opened to the banquet room, you seated yourself anywhere you wanted. There were over 1,200 pastors there, so I hurried to the front to get a good seat. We were seated at round tables for eight people.

As the night began, we were asked to introduce ourselves and get acquainted. We started going around the table, and I was first. To my left were two gentlemen who were from Lawton, Oklahoma. I told them I had lived there when Gary was stationed at the Army base there. Then there was Dick Gruber, the head of children's ministries for our denomination. He introduced himself and mentioned that our children had all been together at the Park Crest Youth Ministries when we lived in Springfield, Missouri. I knew that but was surprised he remembered us. Then there were some older ladies to my right. They all introduced themselves and explained that they had just retired from being missionaries for more than fifty years in Nigeria. I was excited when I heard they had been in Nigeria. I asked them if they knew the Ciminos, Ralph and Esther. They were at one time my grandparents' pastors but had left many years ago to be missionaries in Nigeria. The ladies were surprised, and they got excited when I mentioned the Ciminos.

The lady to my immediate right told me that they all were friends and she was having breakfast the next day with Esther Cimino. I was surprised that they, too, had retired and lived there in Springfield. Then the lady to my right began asking me how I knew them. She looked at me as if she had thought of something and asked me what my grandparents' names were. When I told her, she just about came off her chair. She told me, with tears in her eyes, that my grandmother's name hung in her kitchen in Nigeria for many years. Then I was confused. She explained that back when she went on the mission field, the ladies' church groups would embroider their names on kitchen towels, these were "prayer towels." The ladies would make a commitment with their name to pray for the missionaries. Oh, how I wished my grandparents were still living so I could tell them of my meeting. My new friend gave me the Cimino's phone number and encouraged me to call them. After the banquet was over and I went to my car, it hit me, this was why God wanted me to attend the conference. Tears of joy filled my eyes, and I sat there in the dark and cried at how much God must love me; his loved overwhelmed me as I sat there reflecting on the evening and all that had happened. He had orchestrated all the people at that table to be connected to my life in some way. Only God could have done that for me, I was filled to overflowing by his great love.

The next day, I dialed the Cimino's phone number and hung up three times. I held missionaries in such high esteem, and I thought that they are not going to remember me. I would see them each summer they came home from the mission field. I played with their daughters. One summer, they even taught me how to sing "Jesus Loves Me" in Swahili. I dialed the fourth time, and Ralph Cimino answered. I was speechless for a moment and then I told him I was Arthur Penn Marks' granddaughter. He about dropped the phone and started yelling to his wife, Esther. He told her to come quick, "You will never guess who I am talking to." I was shocked that he thought I was that important. We planned to meet the next day for lunch. There was a blizzard the next day. I thought to myself that these two older people who had lived in Africa for the last fifty-plus years are not going to drive in this weather to see me. I had not heard from them, so I headed to the restaurant, not expecting them to come. To my surprise, they beat me there and were waiting for me.

We had a wonderful time of talking about their African adventures, but what thrilled me most was the stories they told me about my grandparents. It seemed that my grandfather was Ralph's right-hand man when he was my grandparents' pastor. So much so that my grandfather even drove Ralph and Esther to the hospital to have their first child when Ralph could not get his car started, it was out of gas. They told me stories about my grandparents I had never heard. I realized after that meeting that I had an awesome Pentecostal heritage. My grandparents, who had never left the county in Missouri where they were born, knew and supported missionaries around the world. My grandfather wove rugs on a loom he had built himself and sold them to supplement their income after he and my grandmother had retired. They had rugs in many countries around the world. They would send them to missionaries they supported as "prayer rugs." Esther even brought a picture of them from one summer at a potluck meal in their honor given at my grandparents' church. What she did not realize was that my sister and I were in that picture! God is so incredibly good, oh, how he loves you and me. He had put it in my spirit to attend the conference and then arranged for me to meet all these special people. I had never felt God's love so completely envelop me as I did at that moment in time.

God will always challenge us to do the hard things in life. He used my trip to the conference to remind me of his love for me and the wonderful Christian heritage I had and never really understood completely.

What I have learned from my walk with the Lord, over the years, is that he will always ask us to do hard things in life. When he asks, he has a reason, and usually that reason is to help us grow in our faith. When God asks you to do something hard, you will always benefit from the lesson he will teach you. In my life, I have found that God loves me and desires for me to live an abundant life, full of his mercy and grace. I choose to listen and follow him in whatever he asks me to do. My human nature still wants to question why sometimes, but God is patient with us and forgiving when we miss the mark! We must always strive to do better with each new test or assignment. As we run our race in life, we must keep our eyes on Christ and never grow weary in well doing. Face each hard thing God asks you to do with a sense of expectancy. Expect to give it everything you have! Expect to fail sometimes. Expect to be forgiven. Expect to do better with each new challenge God gives you. And expect to grow stronger, more courageous, and victorious in this life here on earth. Run your race to win and never give up because the stakes are too high. To win, you must keep your eyes on the prize and your focus always eternal. Remember, God's word says we are more than conquerors!

## Writing This Book

The writing of this book is another hard thing God has asked me to do. When the idea came to me, I thought it was just my own. When God is pursuing you, he is relentless, and I am thankful for that in my life. He kept speaking to my heart about the need for a book about "suffering." The body of Christ needs to understand suffering to walk in victory. Like always, God and I had a discussion on why it would be impossible for me to write a book. And my list began, I am not an author, I do not know the first thing about writing a book, it will never get published, and so on! Like I said, God is relentless, so here I am writing a book. I do not know if it will ever be published, I just know I need to be obedient.

Every hard thing God asks us to do has a purpose and a blessing. The hard things in life are what change us and stretch our faith and takes us to places we never dreamed possible. When we are obedient, God can work miracles.

## Why the Chaplaincy?

It is always easier to understand looking back at why God might have asked you to do something. As I look back now over the last ten-plus years of our lives. it all seems to come into focus. And as it comes into focus, my faith grows, and I am made stronger.

Let me give you an example of the big picture. God called Gary into the chaplaincy because he was the man for the job. But also because he knew Gary's heart, and I had never seen Gary so happy in his calling as in the chaplaincy. I am so glad he got to do what he loved for those last few years.

But here is the miraculous part of all of it. If Gary had not been obedient to the call to the chaplaincy, we would still be pastoring a church somewhere. If we had been at our last church when Gary got sick, we would have had to leave our home since our home was owned by the church. We would have been without income because the church, understandably, would have needed to hire a new pastor. And we would not have health insurance since the church took care of that. But instead, God had us in the best position we could have been in when Gary got sick. The chaplaincy ministry continued to pay Gary's salary. We lived in our home, so we were not uprooted. And in Virginia, Gary was eligible at the VA for twenty-hours-a-week nursing care. At the VA hospital in DC, where our last church was located, there is no home care provided. As you look at what God did, it was totally amazing and calculated in our favor. Once again, he showed himself strong on our behalf and blessed us beyond anything we would have ever even known to ask for. That is why we need to always trust God to have our best interests in mind. He wants to bless us and take care of us, but we need to trust and obey!

My oldest daughter, Deanna, writes the following on this subject.

## "We Are Called to Do Hard Things"
## by Deanna Tingwald-Higgins

This year, we have endured some very tragic and difficult circumstances because of this God has been teaching me some extremely critical spiritual lessons. One of them is that we are *called to do hard things.*

I thought about so many larger-than-life examples in the Bible of people doing hard things. The Bible is filled from cover to cover with inspirational stories of perseverance, faith, and courage. But I have really been thinking a lot about young Esther. Esther was called to do something remarkably hard that required sheer bravery, skilled planning, and ultimately displayed a deep love for her people. This young inexperienced girl found herself in a role she did not want as queen and in a situation that required exceptional bravery. So much so that an entire book of the Old Testament was named after her and told her story.

I was reading through the book of Esther recently, hoping to gain fresh insight on how she was able to face her problem head on with such strength, grace, and wisdom. Esther was a Jewish orphan being raised by her uncle Mordecai; she was thrown unwillingly into the role of queen because of her beauty after her predecessor was disobedient to the king's orders and was dethroned. Esther was a Jew; the king was Persian and unaware of his new bride's Jewish heritage. Because of some bad advice from the king's most powerful advisor, Haman, the king agreed to destroy the Jews in all the empire. Haman's hatred for the Jews was simple because of Mordecai's love for God and refusal to bow down to Haman.

Mordecai asked Esther to approach the king on behalf of all the Jews facing annihilation and ask for the king to revoke his decree. Unfortunately for Queen Esther, it was a variable death sentence to approach the king without being summoned. Many amazing circumstances happen throughout the rest of the story. Spoiler alert! Esther lives, and she and her uncle both find extraordinary favor with the king, and the Jewish people are saved while their persecutor, Haman, is not. Please read the book of Esther, you will love it!

It is a short but intense book in the Old Testament, one that has many twists and turns. There's extreme irony in the conclusion, and God uses a young, naive, probably "scared out of her mind" Jewish girl to save her people. I came up with a couple of observations about this story of Esther and her calling to do hard things.

First, there was *preparation*. Esther was orphaned and raised by her uncle Mordecai who taught her to love God above all else. Once Esther was chosen to be presented to the king, she had to go through a long twelve-month process of beauty preparations. During this time, she found favor with Haggai, the eunuch in charge of the concubines, and the Bible tells us, "With everyone else who saw her." She ultimately won the favor of the king, and she was chosen to be his queen.

Mordecai finds out about the plot to kill the Jews and goes into a time of desperately seeking God's help. Scripture tells us he goes through a period of fasting and prayer. I cannot think of a better way to prepare for the challenge that lie ahead.

Second, there was *obedience*. Esther obeyed Mordecai when he asked her to approach the king on behalf of all the Jewish people. She clearly was frightened at the thought but trusted Mordecai and ultimately obeyed God's will for her in that moment of terror. I love the fact that she listened to Mordecai and had confidence in his wise counsel. Esther knew that her survival rested on her faith and in her God to save her; she understood the importance of being prepared for the challenge. It was crucial that she be obedient to God and to Mordecai, who gave her sound advice and a divine call to action. Without the strategic timing of the events that unfolded, the king would not have accepted Esther into his courts, and sadly thousands of Jewish men, women, and children would have been slaughtered.

Esther was not hasty in her reaction to the potential destruction of her people, but she was methodical and let the Lord guide her. She took each step of her interaction with the king and her adversary, Haman, very carefully, not wanting to get ahead of God's plan. How many times do we find ourselves in a challenging situation and just want out? Oftentimes thinking we know better than God and do not want to wait around for his timing because it is just too hard. The most well-known verse in the book of Esther is found in chapter 4 verse 14, "For if you remain silent at this time, relief and deliverance for the Jews will arise from another place, but you and your father's family will perish. And who knows but that you come to your royal position for such a time as this?"

God has called us to do hard things. If we are followers of Christ, we will be challenged in our faith, possibly even persecuted. We will face times of terrible suffering and pain. But have we gone through the process of preparation? I think that is the key, it is not if trials come, it is when. When hard times come, are we prepared to face them? Have we studied scripture and know God's word in our heart? Are we active in our relationship with Christ and with those around us that can help us in our spiritual journey? There will be times that we will need to fast and pray desperate prayers.

God placed Esther in a position of leadership to fulfill his plan of saving the Jews in peril. Esther was tasked with embarking on a journey that would most likely end her life. She was called to do something extraordinarily hard, choosing between possible death for herself and that of her people. She listened and obeyed those wiser and older than her, Mordecai spent time fasting and praying, and they were both obedient to God and his perfect timing. Do not be afraid to do hard things, be spiritually prepared for difficult circum- stances and be obedient to God's timing.

## Preparation for Success

In the story of Esther, as my daughter pointed out, we must be prepared and obedient. We need to be prepared *before* the difficult circumstance presents itself. Esther had been brought up by a godly uncle who had taught her the word of God. He taught her to trust and obey God even when she may not fully understand or know the outcome.

We never know what our obedience or disobedience will cost someone else. If Esther had not been obedient, it could have cost the entire Jewish nation to be slaughtered. But because she had been taught to trust and obey God, she saved not only her life but the lives of an entire nation.

When we look back on our life, how many times can we see where our lack of preparation or obedience cost us as well as others? I am certain we each can see things we wish we had done or not done. A job we should have taken or one we should not have taken. A financial decision that was made in haste without praying or seeking wise counsel. We all have times in our lives where we would like to get a "do-over." Even though that is not possible, we can choose to be better prepared and obedient for the next time. How do we get prepared?

*First, by spending time with God and the study of his Word.* We will not know God's direction if we do not know his word. The Word of God is our blueprint for life. In God's Word, we will find answers, direction, correction, instructions on life, and examples on how to live a holy life and so much more. We will discover who God is and how much he loves us. In his Word, we will find comfort, peace, joy, grace, and forgiveness. We cannot rely only on what you hear on Sunday mornings and from others. God desires to speak to "your" heart.

*Second, we need to pray and seek God's will.* We must get alone with God daily and listen as well as pray. Spend some time thanking God for all he has done for you. Then praise God for who he is and all that he is to you. And after a time of thanking and praise, make your needs known to God and always take the time to just sit quietly and listen to God speak to your heart. Have a journal and pen ready to write down God's message to you. Prayer is simply a conversation with God. Just like we talk to one another, there is a time to listen and receive. God desires time with you. He longs to lavish his love on you. Never allow your life to get too busy and rob your daily time with God. When you spend time with God, you will have a more productive day. And always remember that the eternal things in life are accomplished through prayer.

*Third, surround yourself with godly and wise friends you can go to for advice.* Just like in the story of Esther where she had her uncle Mordecai. We need people in our life that we can go to and trust for godly advice. It is not the number of friends you have that matters. It is having a few friends you know you can always trust to speak truth in your life, even when it is not what you want to hear. It is the friend that loves you enough and is not afraid to be honest with you. Statistics say that the average adult will make more than 35,000 decisions in an average day! Our decisions carry consequences, both good and bad. So, having a little help from a friend is vitally important in our lives. Of course, we always want to rely the most on God and his word for our decisions. But there are times when we just need a little extra input from someone we can trust to give us sound advice.

# Obedience for Life Abundant

*It is important that we walk in obedience* to be ready for trials and suffering. Obedience that can only come from knowing God (having a personal relationship with God), knowing the Word of God, and living the Word of God (practicing the Word, being a doer). Before we have to deal with suffering, we must know that it is not if it will come but knowing that the Word of God warns us to be ready because *we will all face suffering* at some time in our life.

"Blessed are those who hear the Word
of God and obey it." (Luke 11:28)

So many of us are left with the misconception at our conversion that life will now be without trouble because God will remove all the trouble in our life and make everything wonderful. But the truth is that the enemy of our soul, Satan, will be furious at our conversion. He will be out to kill, steal, and destroy us! There is still good news... Jesus died so that we might have life and have it even more abundant.

"The thief comes only to steal and kill and
destroy; I have come that they may have life and
have it to the full (abundant)." (John 10:10)

God will not remove all suffering from our lives, but he does promise to be with us every step of the way. And if we will follow God's narrow path of salvation, we will have eternal life. If we do not, we are doomed to hell and torment for eternity. So, any suffering we have now is not too great a price to pay for eternity with God. Jesus had to endure the ultimate suffering for our sins and for our salvation. He paid the price so we can have hope and a future in heaven.

"Enter through the narrow gate. For wide
is the gate and broad is the road that leads
to destruction, and many enter through
it. But small is the gate and narrow is

the road that leads to life, and only a
few find it." (Matthew 7:13–14)

## Loving Care and Trust

I am reminded of the loving care Gary always gave me from the very start of our married life. Because of his protection and care I trusted and would follow him anywhere. I knew that he always had my best interests in mind because he loved me. God is like that with his children, and because of his love and care, we can trust him with our life.

When Gary and I first got married, we lived in northern Iowa where there was a lot of snow. I remember Gary would always walk in front of me if there was not a path already to make my way easier. If I followed in his path, I got along fine. If I did not pay attention and veered off of his path, the way was difficult, and I would most likely slip and fall in the deep snow.

God has made a way for us to follow because of his great love for us. But the way is a narrow path that we must be careful to follow. Like Gary's path made by his love and care for me, God's path is made the same. He loves us and wants all of us to make it to the end of our journey and our faith's goal of heaven! But to be successful at our goal, we must stay on God's narrow path. Living the Christian life is not easy, it takes faith, courage, and determination. We must make our choice and be determined to live for God no matter what.

# CHAPTER 7

## *Eternal Perspective*

He has made everything beautiful in his time.
He has also set eternity in the human heart, yet
no one can fathom what God has done from the
beginning to end.

—Ecclesiastes 3:11

## Eternal Perspective

WHEN YOU HAVE had any kind of traumatic experience, like our family's seven-year battle with ALS, your perspective on life changes. Your views on what is important in life and what is not suddenly take on new meaning. You begin to understand life from an eternal perspective. God has put eternity into our hearts. He has placed within our DNA a desire and hope for things eternal. Yet his word tells us also that no one can fathom eternity. He has placed the desire in us, but it still is difficult for our finite minds to understand eternity. In our lives here on earth, we are all about time and space. We live by our clocks and calendars as our measure of time. Yet eternity is measureless, it is forever. It will go on and on without end. We cannot even digest the depths of God's eternity. Yet somehow, eternity has been made known to us in our hearts. Even heaven and earth, as we now know it, will someday be changed and renewed by God, and we will live forever on this new heaven and new earth. God's Word is from everlasting to everlasting, which means it is eternal—without end and never changing!

I have always known about and believed in eternity in heaven but not given it a lot of thought. That is until Gary, the love of my life, was given a terminal diagnosis. Then eternity seemed very real and very near at hand. That got my attention and caused me to think much more about eternity and what it means for us. We don't like to think about it, but we all will die someday. Only God knows the number of days to our life. We do not give that a lot of thought until something brings it into a clearer focus.

## GG's Funeral—Running Your Best Race

When Gary's Mom died in 2010, we all gathered for her funeral. The minister met with us, and we all spent time together talking about GG's life (GG is what we called her since she was a great grandma). We each shared personal stories about her, many we had never heard before. Things she had done that made her special to each of us. At the funeral, the minister who did not know GG captured her life perfectly through her family's eyes. He likened her life to a race. Gary and I knew that GG was born again because she had discussed it with us. The minister talked about her life and then challenged each of us to take the baton she was passing and run our best race. I have been at many funerals in my life, but I could not tell you what any of the messages were about, but I will always remember the message preached at GG's funeral.

We all have a race to run. You must train and train some more to run a marathon. You don't just get up one morning and say I am going to run a 5K today without working up to the run by training daily. Our life in Christ is like that, we need to be faithful in the things that matter for eternity. Things like *reading the Word of God* daily and putting it into practice in our life. We need to be *prayerful* in everything so that we will hear clearly from God on the direction he has for us. God tells us that we are to *love one another*. We are to *serve each other gladly*. We also need to be *witnessing to the lost* and dying world like laid out for us in the great commission. Each day, it is important that we *praise God* and show him our *thanks* for all he has done for us. And in all these things, we must remain faithful to the one who redeemed us and calls us his own. If we are to run our best race, we must incorporate all these things into our daily life.

I can hear some of you right now, saying who has that kind of time? My response is this, how many hours each day do you spend watching television, browsing Facebook, surfing the Internet, playing video games, and talking on your phone? We need to have our Bibles as near as our cell phones and spend as much time reading our Bibles as we spend on the Internet. If we were honest, we all have the time if we get our priorities straight. I say all that because God has dealt with me about how I waste time. It only takes less than fifteen minutes in the morning to read a devotion and pray. You can witness during the day and set aside some time each month to visit the sick and do a service project. We are all given the same amount of time each day, how will you invest in eternity? We waste so much time doing things each day that have no eternal value.

The Word tells us this about
storing up our treasures:

"Do not store up for yourselves treasures
on earth where moths and vermin destroy
and where thieves break in and steal. But
store up for yourselves treasures in heaven
where thieves do not break in and steal.
For where your treasure is, there your
heart will be also." (Matthew 6:19–21)

We need to always check our motive and purpose in how we are investing our time, talent, and finances. Rev. Billy Graham said it this way, "Give me a minute with a person's checkbook, and I will tell you where their heart is." When we get to heaven, we will be rewarded according to eternal investments we have made during life here on earth. It is important that we think about eternity since we will all be spending the rest of our existence either in heaven or hell.

The other day, I was at a business, and one of the owners was bragging to a customer that he *wanted* to go to hell because that was where all his friends would be. He was just so flippant and arrogant about the whole issue that it broke my heart. I thought to myself, he does not know what he is saying. Hell is not going to be a party with our friends. It is an eternity spent in a horrible existence of suffering and pain, separated from the presence of God, and so much worse than we can comprehend. Listening to that conversation made me want to go stand on the street corner and yell out "Jesus loves you and wants you to be with him in heaven." It made me think about my eternal investment in souls. When we get to heaven, I believe all those whose lives we have touched with the gospel will be waiting for us at heaven's gate. I do not know about you, but I pray to see thousands waiting for me to the glory of the Father and his kingdom.

## Our Responsibility

I have mentioned this in other chapters but want to, once again, bring it to your attention. We are all responsible for our understanding of the Word of God. We cannot afford to leave the foundation of our faith to others. Parents, you are responsible to teach your children the truth of God's Word, don't leave it up to Sunday school-teachers and the pastor of your church. It is vitally important to your child's eternity that they know and understand God's Word. Your best lesson is a life lived as an example of the Word and a reflection of Christ. When your children see you making God's Word a priority in your life, they too will develop a love and desire to read the Word.

Did you know that the Word of God tells us that we will be held accountable for every word we have ever spoken?

"But I tell you that everyone will have to give account on the day of judgment for every empty word they have spoken. For by your words

you will be acquitted, and by your words you
will be condemned." (Matthew 12:36–37)

I don't know about you, but when I first read this verse, it struck remorse in my heart. We will be judged by our own words. How often have I spoken without thought of the consequences? And how many empty words have I said? Too many to remember, but God has a record. We thought the computer was an awesome invention. How amazing is it that God has record of our every word? It is our responsibility to search and study the scriptures so that we know what is important and what is not. We want to know what breaks God's heart so we can pray that it will break our heart too. We do not have to be Bible scholars, but we do need to be aware of what God's Word teaches. As believers the Word of God tells us this,

"Therefore, there is now no condemnation for
those who are in Christ Jesus." (Romans 8:1)

As Christians, our sins have been forgiven by Christ's death on the cross, but we will receive rewards according to the eternal investments we have made. The book of Revelation puts it this way,

"Look, I am coming soon! My rewards is
with me, and I will give to each person
according to what they have done."

When we die and meet God, he will either greet us with, "Well done, thy good and faithful servant" (Matthew 25:21), and you will be ushered into heaven to receive your rewards. Or you will be greeted by God saying, "Depart from me, I never knew you" (Matthew 7:23), and you will be cast into hell.

It is important that we weigh our works on God's scale. Owning your own home, your success in a career, your earthly awards, the car you drive will not be rewarded in heaven. Sharing the gospel with the lost, giving to missions, tithing, acts of kindness and service are all things that God will reward us for. It is my fear that so much we do, even in what we see as ministry, will go unrewarded because God will look at our heart condition. For myself, I must ask, "Did I do it as a people pleaser to be recognized, or did I do it in secret, wanting no recognition?" We must always be aware of our motives and the condition of our heart. I want to receive as many rewards in heaven as possible because the Bible says we will lay them at the feet of Jesus. It will be all we will have to offer him. I want to offer him as much as possible because he has done so much for me.

## The Swing of the Pendulum

In my life, I have experienced a huge swing in the pendulum of preaching styles. In my grandparents' church when I was young, in the '50s, the preacher yelled a lot about hell. People got saved lots of time out of fear of hell. That was not a bad thing if they were sincere. In those days, you did not hear as much about the softer side of the gospel message like we do today.

I also remember that in the '50s, the church was very legalistic and called almost everything sin or evil. It was considered a sin in my grandparents' church for women to wear jeans or slacks. It was considered a sin to wear any kind of makeup. It was considered a sin to own a television or dance. I could go on and on with this list, but I will stop. Some of these things, like the women and slacks, was also a cultural thing. I wore dresses to school until I was in junior high. It was just what you did in the fifties.

Today, the church gets caught up in the trappings of being politically correct or relevant. That cracks me up because Jesus was relevant but never tried to fit in with the world. His life message opposed the world and the spiritual leaders of his day. He never tried to change his message to suit the times, and his message is still the same today. We need to be very careful of what we call right and wrong and what we think the church needs to look like to attract the lost. We just need to stick to the scriptures that are eternally unchanging and relevant always. We can have coffee bars, offer food, fellowship, and special features, there is nothing wrong with that. But what attracts people and keeps them coming back is the presence of God and feeling loved and accepted from the front door of the church until the last amen.

I remember at one of the churches that we pastored, there was a family from another denomination who started attending. They had a lot of problems with the doctrines of our church denomination. Because of that, Gary would not allow the husband to hold a teaching position in the church. One day, he came into Gary's office and confronted Gary about the situation. Gary explained his position on the matter and then asked the man, "Why is your family coming to the church and why have they stayed?" He simply answered, "Because we feel the presence of God and love here." With all the differences, they stayed because they felt the spirit of God and his love in the church!

## Do-Overs

We know living a holy life starts with a change on the inside of us, not on our outward appearance. Our clothes, makeup, and hair do not make us holy. It is our love for God that will bring the inside "heart change" that we all so desperately need.

Never give up because there is always tomorrow. God's love and forgiveness is new every morning. You can start with a clean slate everyday if need be until you have success. In our family, we call that a "do-over." We all need do-overs in our life because we are not perfect. God will always be right there to pick you up, dust you off, and set your feet on the solid rock one more time!

God wants us to know the full truth of the gospel message. His heart is for us to be transformed by his love that he desires to lavish on us. We must come to salvation knowledge in reverence and respect because of Jesus shed blood on the cross and his amazing grace, pardon, and forgiveness. His Father's heart wants us to know freedom from sin and shame. Our heavenly Father desires for us to realize the full potential of the authority given us in the name so we can walk in victory. The power in his son's shed bled will help reveal the truth in his Holy Word. But that is still not the "full gospel" story. It is important that we know about the place he is preparing for all who choose the narrow road, it is heaven. Heaven is a beautiful place filled with God's love, glory, grace, and presence. A place with streets of gold and a crystal sea. A place where the gate we will enter through is made from one large pearl!

But there is more to his story. He wants us to also understand that he is a jealous God who wants no other God but him in our life. He wants us to put him before our spouse, family, and friends. He also warns us in his word that he will punish the world for their sin. He warns of his wrath and that he has a place called hell for all who do not choose him. Hell is a place of everlasting punishment and separation from God.

We serve a Holy God that calls us to be holy as he is holy. That does not mean we will be perfect. That is why we need a Savior. But it does mean God wants us to do our best to live a holy life. A life where we are constantly in forward movement, being changed daily more into the Father's likeness. He desires us to live for him in such a way that our life will glorify him and bring others to the saving knowledge of our Lord Jesus Christ.

Heaven and hell are real places. Some teaching is out there that everyone will go to heaven because God is love. They fail to read the scriptures about God's judgment and wrath. God is just and fair, and sin will not go unpunished. Hell is described as a lake of fire with no relief from the heat or flames, a place of eternal pain and suffering with no way out. Jesus talked a lot about hell, but today in our pulpits, it is hardly ever mentioned. God's Word tells us that hell is a real place. It is a place where physical bodies and souls will be cast into what is called outer darkness, forever separated from God. Jesus taught that both the earthly body and soul would be eternally destroyed in hell. It is a place of loneliness, hopelessness, and terror. Hell is a place for those who did not choose to follow Christ and live for him.

God desires that all would be saved, but it remains our choice. Jesus had to descend into hell to defeat Satan for your sins and mine. Our salvation is a gift from God to us, but we must always remember that Christ paid the price with his life! It is not something we could earn or ever be found worthy to receive. Our only boast is in

Christ alone who paid the price. But even though God desires all to be saved, he is still a God of justice who demands sin's price to be paid. When we accept Jesus as our Savior and Lord, we are instantly a brand-new creation, the old man/nature is crucified with Christ, and God makes us a brand-new creation in him. Christ paid sin's price for us. From the moment of our salvation, God will renew our minds as we live for him. He will change our old sin nature into a new creature in Christ. We are no longer slaves to sin. Salvation is instant, but our renewing happens daily as we read his Word and find out who we are because of Christ Jesus. We are known as Christians by our love and what we do, our actions and how we live our life out daily before God and man. Jesus tells us the mystery in Mark,

> "Whoever wants to be my disciples must deny themselves and take up their cross and follow me. For whoever wants to save their life will lose it, but whoever loses their life for me and for the gospel will save it." (Mark 8:35)

## My Personal Testimony

I still remember the moment Christ saved me, pulled me out of the pit, and set my feet on the solid rock. The very foundation of my life was set that day. It was the summer I was ten years old when I got saved. I was not from a family that went to church. I always knew my parents loved and believed in God but never saw them attend church or really live for God. My father was an alcoholic, and my mother had been raised by an alcoholic father after her mother's death when my mom was only three years old. Side note to this story: my grandmother (my mother's mom) was a circuit riding preacher back in the thirties. She was ahead of her time!

Each summer, my brothers and sisters and I would spend the entire summer vacation with my grandparents. They lived about four hours away from us. The summer I was ten, I stayed there by myself for some reason. The boys were getting too old, I guess, and my older sister stayed home to help Mom with my youngest sister. There were five of us, I was fourth, in birth order. My grandparents lived in a little Missouri town, and their lives revolved around the church. We went to church on Sunday morning, Sunday evening, and on Wednesday night. That summer, there was a weeklong revival being held at their Assembly of God church. Every night at this revival, I was drawn to the altar call at the end of each service but was too shy to get up and go. On the last night at the altar call, I do not even remember walking up to the altar, the next thing I knew, there I stood praying and waiting for prayer.

The preacher came to my end of the altar, where I stood, and laid his hands on my forehead and began to pray for salvation. I asked Jesus into my heart, and the next thing that happened surprised us all, I was filled with the baptism in the Holy Spirit and began to speak in tongues. Now I didn't even know what tongues were, but I still remember that moment like it happened yesterday. It has been more than sixty years, but I remember feeling like I had a direct line to heaven and I was talking to God without knowing what I was saying. I felt like God was cleaning me from the inside out. That was the moment of my first look at eternity. I stood there like that speaking in tongues for about thirty minutes. My grandma was not there that night because she was not feeling well. When we got home, my grandpa told me to tell grandma what had happened, so I told her that I got saved. But grandpa seemed to be more excited about me being filled with the baptism. I was confused because I felt that the most important thing that happened was my salvation. I found out later that my grandfather had been seeking the baptism but had not yet been filled.

Over the years, I have thought a lot about why God filled that little ten-year-old girl with and overflowing amount of his precious Spirit. I believe what God has taught me is that I needed the extra power to live my life in the environment I would go home to. My older sister and I always attended church, but sadly, I did not serve God like I should have in my teens. We had no guidance or Christian influence in our home, and that did not help our situation. My best friend, Debbie, from fifth grade and to this day had a positive influence on my life. Her family always went to church together, and I remember thinking, *When I have a family, I want to make sure we all go to church together.* God used her family as a witness to me and to plant that seed of faith and desire in my life.

When Gary and I had our first child, we started going to church as a family and never stopped. I remember what a man in our church said the day we dedicated Deanna, "This child will never remember a time she was not in church." Gary got saved, and I rededicated my life to Christ and was once again filled with an overflowing of God's precious Holy Spirit. This was where our cornerstone in Christ was set and our true foundation laid for our future. That was the beginning of our walk with God that has lasted over fifty years.

Side note to my salvation story: I went home that summer, and when I got back to school, I shared with my best friend, Debbie, about what had happened, even the baptism of the Holy Spirit. She did not go to a church that believed in the baptism of the Holy Spirit. But years later, her husband became a pastor, and they got filled with the baptism of the Holy Spirit. She said that it helped because I had shared my experience with her so many years before, so she was open to the infilling. She and her husband had to change denominations because of the infilling. I say that so the reader will understand that it was not an easy decision to make when your husband is a pastor and you need to change denominations for your belief. But the infilling of God's Spirit is worth it all. We never know when we share about God's goodness how it plants seed in the heart and grow many years later. Our God does the impossible!

## Gary's Salvation

Gary has a similar story. His family basically attended church on Christmas and Easter. He went to church some as a child but not on a regular basis. Since I wasn't living for God when we met, I was not concerned or even knew to be concerned that he was not saved. Just six months after we met, we were married. And six months after we were married, he was drafted into the Army and sent to the Republic of Vietnam to fight for our country. While he was in Vietnam, he took part in the invasion of Cambodia. They were flown into Cambodia by helicopter. The helicopter in front of the one Gary's group was on crashed in the jungle. The commanding officer of Gary's group told them to jump and run when their helicopter got close to the ground.

Gary and three other men were separated from their company as they jumped and ran. They were lost in the jungles of Cambodia and surrounded by the enemy for three days and nights. During their time in the jungle, Gary prayed and told God that if he would save their lives, he would live for him forever. Gary was able to save the three men that were with him and get them reunited with their company. The men that Gary saved requested he be given an honor for saving their lives; Gary received a Bronze Star for Valor for his heroic service. When your life is held in the balance, you are given eternal perspective, and that is where Gary's perspective changed. When Gary got home, without telling me about his promise to God, he started going to church with me and accepted Christ as his personal Savior in 1972 during a Lay Witness Mission at our church. Gary was true to the promise he had made to God. He served God the rest of his life and was strong in his faith; even when his body was failing at the end, his faith never wavered.

## Forever Focused on Eternity

Now that I have a clearer understanding of where my focus should be directed, I will forever strive to keep my motives and purpose in sync with God's will for my life. Our life here on earth is just a vapor, here today and gone tomorrow. I am more concerned than ever about my daily walk with God. I want to make every moment count for eternity. Let us be about our Father's business of winning souls, serving and working for the kingdom, and ever-growing and maturing to become more like Jesus. Our goal needs always to be, as we love and serve others, Christ will be seen in us. It is not important for us to be remembered but more important to bring glory and honor to Christ and have him remembered for all generations.

The Apostle Paul reminds us that in the last days, it will be difficult for us. We know sin will be greater even though it is hard to imagine things being worse than they are now. God's Word tells us that we will suffer more than Paul. That is not a great picture of our future, but God tells us so we will not get caught by surprise but be ready when the trials come.

> "People will be lovers of themselves, lovers of money, boastful, proud, abusive, disobedient to their parents, ungrateful, unholy, without love, unforgiving, slanderous, without self-control, brutal, not lovers of the good, treacherous, rash, conceited, lovers of pleasure rather than lovers of God." (2 Timothy 3:2–4)

## Reading God's Word with Eternal Perspective

When God touches your life and opens your eyes to his heart, you will see things differently. I used to read my Bible just to see what I could get out of it for me. It was an attitude like going to church to be blessed instead of going to church to be a blessing! Now I read the Word to find out more about the God I love. It is amazing how God will give you new insight into his word when you read it looking for him and not just for yourself. If we are to be his reflection to others, we need to know more about the person we are to reflect. When we read to seek more of God revealed, we will understand so much more. We will begin seeing through God's eyes. That will turn your priorities upside down!

## Your New Focus

With this new focus, you will become much more conscious of God's presence in your life because he has begun to fill your thought life. You start evaluating the world through eternity.

Loving others with the 1 Corinthians 13 kind of love becomes your motive. And making eternal investments is now your purpose. Your choices in life have changed. You now love others without expecting anything in return. And there is no fear of rejection in your love. You find it easier to forgive and get on with life. Your giving takes a new depth of generosity and eternal hope. You give without any strings attached. You give from your heart, not your bank account. You give because you know God's rewards are so much better than anything the world has to offer. You give to make eternal investments. Investments that moth and flames cannot destroy.

Your new focus on eternity changes who you want to become. Being important by the world's standards is not what you seek. You don't want or need to be great, you just want to do great things for God's kingdom. You desire to be led moment by moment by God's will and design for your life because you now realize how much God has planned for you. You are filled with a passion and a purpose that only God can fulfill in your life. You now realize that we are all given twenty-four hours in a day, but the amount of time given us is not as critical as what we do with that time and how we make eternal investments. God has given us all gifts, and we need to be about the Father's business using our gifts for his kingdom. You may think you are not gifted, but you are. Most of us think of gifts like singing, speaking, dancing, playing an instrument. We all have gifts, here are mine: I am an organizer, I am an encourager, I have the gift of hospitality, I can speak and write, I have a license and a car, and I like to cook—now I didn't say I was a great cook, but I can cook! So, I will use all those gifts and more to bring glory to my heavenly Father and his kingdom. We all have gifts or ways to further God's kingdom; we just must find them and ask God how he wants us to use them for him.

Our age does not matter; if we have the desire to be used, God will use us in his kingdom. Over our years of ministry, I have heard so many reasons why people can't serve. One that I never understood, or maybe I should be honest and say agreed with, was I am too old and I've already done my part with listing all they have done since they were three! God can use *all* of us. When we get older, what we can do may change, but we can all do something. You can sit at home and make calls, send cards, and pray. If you have a car and can drive, you can visit people. If you can still breathe, *serve God* in some capacity. We can never do enough for God because he has done so much for us. Serve him willingly and joyfully.

I saw Gary from his hospital bed when he could not talk, walk, eat, or breathe, but still serve God. He would pray for people and our family using his iPad for speech. He encouraged all who came to visit him. He even served communion to a group of men from his bed without saying a word but using his iPad! None of us there will ever forget that communion service. He worshipped God with others from his bed. No one who came into our home ever left the same after an encounter with Gary and his God. So, please do not give excuses when your asked, better yet, do not wait to be asked, volunteer!

# CHAPTER 8

## *Grieving and Counting My Blessings*

Blessed are they that mourn for they will be comforted.

—Matthew 5:4

### Our Bedroom Where Gary Saw Jesus

AT SOME POINT in Gary's illness, our bedroom was transformed into a hospital room. All the equipment he needed for his care seemed to take over the room that had been just a resting place before. It was all now a part of the journey we were on. The bedroom became our place to live our lives. In our bedroom, we read God's word and prayed, we greeted friends and family there, we laughed, we cried, and we fell more in love with one another and our sweet Savior, and it was where we said our goodbyes. It was in that same room we became so much more eternally minded and aware of what life was all about. When you are confronted with a terminal illness, you learn to cherish every moment you have and to make the most of every day you have left together. Our bedroom was a sacred place where we lived out those last precious moments of life with one another and our loved ones. It was there that we shared our love, our hopes, and our dreams. It was in that room our grandchildren came to spend time with their sweet grandpa for the last time. They would sit on his bed, love on him, talk to him, sing, and play the ukulele for him. And it was in that very room where Gary saw Jesus and Jesus took him home.

Just a few days before Gary died, we were gathered in the bedroom just laughing and talking while he slept. He slept all the time now. But suddenly, he opened his eyes and looked up at the ceiling. His face and eyes had such a radiant look of recognition that I asked him if he saw Jesus. He turned his head slightly toward me and nodded yes. That was our last communication with him. I have no doubts that God was in that room with us that night. In that room, Gary took his last breath on earth and his first breath in heaven. Angels were in that same room to take him home where his eternal life began. Someone asked me later if it bothered me that he had died in our room. Without hesitation, I shared that my bedroom is the most sacred room in my home and where I find peace in knowing it was there where Gary met his beautiful Savior. What a precious memory that our family can treasure, hold on to, and cherish.

## Life Will Never Be the Same

It was strange how quickly, after Gary died, that our bedroom was transformed back into its original purpose. The hectic daily routine of nurses' visits, aids to shower Gary, and the administering medications, feeding tubes, and trach cleaning all have ceased. Once a busy room with many people in and out every day is now still. I am left to struggle with the deafening silence and loneliness that filled our home. Life will never be the same in that sacred room of ours. The battle for life fought there will never be forgotten. In our room, I still meet with God; he comforts my tears and quiets my heart that is so full of grief. I cling to the blessed hope of seeing Gary again someday. In that I can rejoice! I realize now that our trials here on earth, like our lives, are but a fleeting moment and gone. I am reminded of what Gary said when he was diagnosed, "Vickie, we are all terminal!" Now it is even more important to me to make every moment count for God's kingdom because I know how quickly my life will be over and my work here will be finished. There is an urgency in my life, like never before, an urgency to tell others that they, too, can find victory in the suffering. Because life here will only get harder, and we need to be ready for whatever life brings.

## Life Goes On—Dealing with Grief

Life goes on, somehow; I have not figured it all out just yet. For me, my life will never be the same without Gary. Yet somehow, I know that God is going to show me the way. I need to be patient and wait on the Lord and not get out ahead of his plan for me. My heart will always overflow with sweet memories of a love that not everyone gets to experience in this life. I feel blessed to have had Gary in my life for as long as God gave him to me. Blessed that he was the father to my children and grandfather to their children. He made us all better people for having him in our lives. In some way, he was the best part of me. I have known the love spoken of in 1 Corinthians chapter 13. For all this, I am thankful. I will hold fast to the memories that God has entrusted to me and with them move forward in God's precious love. In our room, I will continue to meet with God and learn how to be more of a reflection of him.

One of the ways God has taught me to deal with my grief is to remember all my blessings. For the first year after Gary died, I kept a journal of what I had to be thankful for. I tried to record at least five blessings each day to keep my heart in tune with God's heart. Here are just a few of the blessings I recorded.

## Thankful for My Blessings

I am thankful for a loving Savior. I am thankful for our blessed hope of heaven. I am thankful for my family and friends. I am thankful for my children who have a heart for God. I am thankful for all the years God gave me with Gary. I am thankful for my grandchildren. I am thankful that Gary and I had time to say our goodbyes. I am thankful that each day I can read God's Word and draw closer to him. I am thankful for knowing God's presence in my life. I am thankful for my salvation. I am thankful to be found worthy to suffer for Christ. I am thankful for knowing God loves me. I am thankful God fights my battles for me. I am thankful for the plans God has for my life, to prosper me and not to harm me and to give me a hope and a future. I am thankful that God is my peace. I am thankful that the Lord is my strength. I am thankful that I am courageous because Christ lives in me.

It was surprising how just focusing on my blessings each day kept me going in the right direction. When we can see the positive in life, it puts everything else into proper perspective. My sweet husband was the most positive person I have ever known. I would like to think some of that rubbed off onto me!

## And God Said "Just Be"

In my grief, I cried out to the Lord, "Lord, my heart aches with more grief than I can bare. I would miss Gary every waking moment. I felt so lost. I did not know what to do with my life now that I was by myself." I wanted to be obedient to God more than ever before, but I was barely making it through each day. I asked God to be my strength, be my courage, and direct me with his love and mercy. "I am glad that Gary is with you, Lord. I am glad he is whole again, and I would not want him to suffer any more. But, please, give me peace and help my hurting heart to stop aching." God answered me and said, "Just be."

My entire life, it seems, I have been in a hurry. Gary was always telling me to slow down so I would not fall—I was a little clumsy, and my "type A" personality did not help. When I was grieving, I felt like I needed to be hearing from God as what to do next. My grandson, Noah, in his wisdom told me, "Grandma, you don't always need to be doing something, just take this time to rest." Those words proved to be just what I needed to hear. God was telling me to take time to grieve, do not rush things. "Just be" for a while. *Be still* and know that I am God. *Be patient* and know I am with you. *Be at rest* for your body, spirit, and soul. *Be at peace*, knowing I will care and guide you in life. *Be calm* and take this time to renew your soul. *'Just be'* and let me carry you for just a little while."

God, in his infinite wisdom, always knows exactly what we need. I needed to hear from God that it was all right to just rest in his love for a while. I had to learn; I could tell the precious ladies at our church that kept inviting me to Bible study that I would come when I felt ready. I had cared for everyone else my whole life, my husband, my children, my friends, my extended family, and my church family. It did not feel right to just care for "me." So, God gave me permission to "just be" for now.

Grief is so unexplainable and unpredictable. You can have a day where you feel like you are going to make it and you are moving forward and then something stirs a memory and you are right back there in that place of grief. Your friends and family try to help because seeing you in your grief is hard for them too. Words, food, cards, and visits help but nothing can take the pain of loss away.

Widow, the first time I had to check that box, I nearly fell apart right there in my doctor's office. And I did not like identifying with the widowed ladies at my church. I loved them, but I just was not ready to join that group. Grief is uniquely felt by each of us. And I have learned that the harder you love, the greater the grief. My husband and I did everything together. We had been in ministry together for over forty years, working side by side and married for almost fifty years. Gary tried to make it to our fiftieth anniversary but died seven months before. We loved being together in everything. We loved serving God and investing in his kingdom. Gary was a true "family man," his family was his life, after his love for Jesus. So, grief hit me hard.

> "He will wipe away every tear from their
> eyes, and death shall be no more, there
> will no longer be any mourning, crying,
> or pain for the old order of things have
> passed away." (Revelation 21:4)

## We Do Not Grieve Like the World Grieves: What Does That Even Mean?

You try to be strong, and as a Christian, you do not ever act like you are losing it because we are not to grieve like the world grieves. But what does that mean? It does not mean that just because you are a Christian, you do not grieve and hurt just as much as someone else. It means that, in our grief, we have the hope that we will see our loved one again someday. It does not make the aching in our hearts any less. God will comfort us and help us, but we need to always be real about our grief.

> "Grief is the last act of love we can give to those we loved. Where there is deep grief, there was great love." (Anonymous)

God will not take all the pain away, but he will walk right beside you and carry you when you cannot take another step. When I am attacked by bouts of grief, I do my best to fight back by putting on praise music and spending some time in the presence of God. It always helps me to get through the worst of the battle. God knows all about grief, and he knows and feels our grief. Jesus suffered every pain, sickness, and disease on the cross for us, for me. So, I know he understands.

> "The pain passes, but the beauty remains." (Pierre Renoir)

So, for now, I will go on living and striving to be the woman of faith that God has called me to be. My determination is solid, and my course is set; I will continue this journey of life for my God, my husband, and my family. God is the strength, my courage, and my reason to run my best race. And I know it is what my sweet husband would desire of me as well. God is not through with me and has other books for me to write about his glory and saving grace. Because of the last few years of my life, I have learned that God only asks us to do the hard things that lead us to greater victories in him!

My oldest daughter, Deanna, shared her experiences with grief in a blog as a healing time for her and in hopes it would help someone else. I would like to share some of her articles with you, let her words bring comfort to your grieving heart and help you in your darkest hour. Whatever you are going through, remember that you are never alone.

## "Life Is Strange Sometimes" by Deanna Tingwald-Higgins

Life is so strange sometimes. I wish my dad wouldn't have spent the last few years of his life the way he did; I wanted him to be able to throw the football with my boys, to wrestle on the floor, and chase them around the house until they were all out of breath from laughter. But that was not the life we were given. To say I spent many hours questioning and wrestling with God would be a gross understatement. Somehow, through the pain and suffering, we had countless holy encounters with our Creator, times that only he was able to issue the strength, courage, and ability we needed to keep moving on this terrifying journey. My faith was reinforced and even invigorated even in the sadness and constant sorrow of loss. It was an unexpected and divine gift that came out of an atrocious season of suffering.

My heavenly Father faced suffering I cannot even imagine. My earthly father faced suffering that I could barely find the courage to watch toward the end. Not only did Jesus endure horrible suffering for us but he chose it. He chose it so that you and I could be free from sin. I do not understand it, but I am humbled and grateful for it.

I choose suffering because it was and is God's plan. I choose suffering because he met me at that place of exhaustion and made me a better follower of him. He used my dad as a beautiful vessel to teach me and countless others the lesson of loving Christ deeper even when suffering.

I live by the ocean. It is beautiful and frightening at the same time. This life is beautiful, but suffering will come, embrace it. Learn from it. Be stronger because of it. Allow Christ to meet you in your most dreadful storm that life will certainly throw at you. My dad did, and he taught me to embrace it through the power of our heavenly Father, the prince of peace.

## "Jesus Is Enough" by Deanna Tingwald Higgins

Today is the anniversary of my dad meeting Jesus face-to-face. What an impossibly glorious thought of what this past year must have been like for my dad as he worshipped his Creator in his new and perfectly whole body, now living in paradise. My heart is over-joyed at the thought of my amazing earthly father residing with my all-powerful and perfectly holy heavenly Father.

I find myself longing to be in such company, along with the angels and all those who have gone before us to their eternal glory worshipping the one true Creator.

Life is full of ups and downs, highs and lows. It just is. Everyone will face moments of absolute joy, finding delight in beautiful moments gifted to us by God, but there will also be devastating set-backs and heartaches to endure.

I have experienced them both. Joy and heartache, delight and devastation. Jesus is in them both. His presence should not be taken for granted, lost, or forgotten in either circumstance, good or bad.

As I have wrestled with my faith the past couple of years I am profoundly strengthened and encouraged because of the battle. I have been embarrassed and ashamed when my reality was one of incredible doubt and endless questions. When I have wavered and asked God the tough questions, God was not mad at me. He did not get offended or flee from me. He showed me mercy when my foundation seemed to be crushing.

In a purely miraculous way, my faith was being restored and strengthened, the struggle and wrestling forced me to deconstruct my faith and start the construction process back to my first love. Jesus has not changed; he is the same yesterday, today, and forever. He is not afraid of my struggle and insecurities; he is right there…in life and in death.

I will never forget the moment I got the phone call about my dad's passing. His death was expected, and we had gathered with him for months just about every day thinking it was the end. We had joked about the fact that we had said our "goodbyes" so many times, my poor dad was probably tired of hearing our "it's okay to go" speech. He had a fabulous sense of humor, and I think that is what I miss the most.

Those days we watched my dad slowly and painfully lose his battle with ALS were long and terrible, they were gut-wrenching. But I have learned many lessons. I have grown in my relationship with my God and my family and the brave friends that stood beside our family when we could barely function. Most of all, I learned that Jesus is enough.

My dad knew that Jesus was enough. He served him faithfully to the end. I know it was not easy for him, I know he wanted to be strong for us. I also know that he chose God even when he may not have felt like it—the end of his life was heartbreaking. It just was. You cannot sugarcoat the ugliness of disease and the isolation of death. He was not able to speak, but I know that he would have proclaimed that Jesus is enough! I know that this was not what he wanted the end of his life to look like, I am sure he had his disappointments. There were tears and times of uncertainty, but Jesus is enough!

If you are struggling with grief, if you are experiencing a terrible life-altering circumstance, please know that it is okay. The struggle is okay. You will grow in the struggle with your faith. Your faith will be strengthened. Please, do not feel guilty but know that God loves you and most importantly that *Jesus is enough*!

## "Celebrating a Life Well-Lived Birthdays in Heaven" by Deanna Tingwald-Higgins

Today, May 22, 2019, is my dad's seventieth birthday. It is a little different for our family now that he is celebrating in heaven. We celebrate his birthday by knowing he is finally able to eat all the ice cream he desires and maybe even partaking in one of his favorite pastimes, playing baseball with some of the greats that have gone before him. If there are rocks to skip in heaven, that may be where you will find my dad. I would like to think that skipping rocks in heaven would be somewhere along the beautiful shoreline filled with the most perfectly shiny, smooth pebbles. Just one flick of the wrist and that pebble would glide across the top of that majestic water, finding its resting place at the bottom of the crystal blue shallows. Or perhaps he is blissfully waiting along the water's edge of some sort of heavenly tropical beach, with the bottoms of his jeans cuffed perfectly so as not to get them wet. "Meet me at the beach" is what he would tell my mom before he died. I guess he wanted my mom to know where to find him when she entered through the pearly gates of heaven.

I cannot think of a better meeting place. If he were here, he would start the day by making a "larger than life" stack of pancakes for the grandkids. Pancakes were about the only culinary delights he would attempt in the kitchen. Cooking was not his thing, but his flapjacks would make the grandkids come running and demanding more. The last several years, we would end the day by taking in a Tide's game, it was his favorite pastime. He was a darn good ball player in his younger days, but his last few birthdays spent at the ball-park were a terrible struggle for him because of the ALS. I remember as a young girl watching him play slow pitch with a ball the size of a grapefruit! I could never figure out they caught that thing, it was ginormous! The last year that he was able to make it to Harbor Park Stadium proved to be an enormously challenging outing for his tired and withering body. As we have just past the one-year mark of his passing and celebrate his birthday today, I have been reflecting so heavily on precious memories that are more valuable than any rare jewel I have been reflecting on grief, trying to process his last seven years on this earth. And I have also been reflecting on what it means to move on, to continue this life without someone you love so dearly.

Grief is a funny thing. I thought when my dad passed on that we would have a sense of relief, that we would start the process of living our lives again. Picking up where we left off, so to speak. But it has not been like that. I guess I thought that we had grieved so much over the seven years and had faced so much loss that possibly those days of sadness were coming to an end. I was wrong. There is so much to process these days that my head spins much of the time. Now that my dad's suffering has stopped, we are relieved, but now what? The sadness that blanketed our family during the first several months after his death was brutal. There were glimpses of hope and happiness that surprised me and caught me off guard at times. I remember being so thankful for those moments that reminded me of the strange thing called "happiness." On the other hand, some days have brought much heaviness and sorrow; trying to wade through and process the many questions felt overwhelming.

Why did we feel so isolated and alone for much of those seven years? How long will we carry this heavy baggage of this terrible loss? There were many wrestling matches with God during the last couple of years of my dad's life. Trying to come to terms with the "whys" but realizing it's really about the "why nots." Now I wrestle to overcome bitterness and overwhelming sadness that come in terrible surges like the powerful but frightening waves of an angry ocean.

Oftentimes, while during our trial, I was embarrassed of my sadness and felt apologetic for my feelings. I do not anymore. I would find myself in places where I should have felt loved, accepted, and safe with my emotions, but instead, I would feel judged, misunderstood, or even disregarded. People would look at me funny or not look at me at all, which was even more painful. I still feel that way much of the time, I really wish I did not. I tried to bury my grief after my dad died, wanting to magically move on and lead a normal life again. I did not understand that after we had been through a never-ending tsunami of suffering, now there is a different kind of grief period.

Today is my dad's first birthday in heaven, so what do I do now? I know that my dad would not want me to stay this way, so I will not. I know that my dad would want me to love people, so I will. My relationship with God is so much more vibrant and purer than it was just a few months ago. Sometimes when God seemed silent and absent in our situation, he was somehow the most present. He was working his greatest, most refining work I could have ever imagined. I do not fully understand the theology behind it, but I just know that "his ways are higher." To go through something like this and not be changed for the better would be calamitous. Thankfully, I feel like my senses are much more attuned to those struggling; when I look into someone's eyes, I want to know their story. I want to know their struggle, their pain, or how they overcame or how I can come alongside them in their journey to provide support.

Although I have many setbacks as I try to traverse grief, bitterness, and loss… I also know that a new day is coming when things will get easier, life will get sweeter, and the world's colors will come back in all their fullness. I also know that one day I will be sitting on the beach with my dad, or maybe watching him play slow pitch again… I will search for the perfect pebble on the heavenly shores of majestic rivers and partake of calorie-free, fat-free deliciously fluffy pancakes. Until then, I will keep living, I will stay on my journey that Christ has set before me, and I will go to Cracker Barrel on my dad's birthdays and order the highest stack of "flapjacks" they have on the menu.

"Grief is not a sign of weakness nor a lack of faith. It is the price we pay for love."

Gary and I kissing while on his R&R from Vietnam

Sept of 1968 our wedding

Gary in our bedroom with grandchildren while having ALS

Gary on our last trip to the Biltmore

Gary and I with all grandkids

# About the Author

VICKIE TINGWALD WAS married in 1968 to her husband, Gary. Gary passed away on February 20, 2018, from a seven-year battle with ALS. Vickie and Gary have four grown children and seven grandchildren. Vickie and Gary were both ministers with the Assemblies of God. They were in ministry together for over forty years. Both grew up in Iowa and came to the East Coast in 1991 to take a church in Crisfield, Maryland.

They pastored churches in Crisfield, Maryland, and Gaithersburg, Maryland, and then they moved to Chesapeake, Virginia, to begin a ministry in the chaplaincy.

Vickie's love of writing led her to write about their family's journey with the terminal illness of ALS. She shares their struggles and what God taught them about suffering and "Finding Joy In The Journey."

CPSIA information can be obtained
at www.ICGtesting.com
Printed in the USA
BVHW030833120323
660253BV00018B/252

9 781662 432385